Where is My Sister?

Pauline A. Brown

Doorlight Publications
Cambridge, Massachusetts | Abington, Pennsylvania
www.doorlightpublications.com

Cover image: Ralph Brown

Cover design: Ruth Anne Burke

ISBN 0-9982233-5-2
ISBN13 978-0-9982233-5-3

Interior Design: Ruth Anne Burke

For Marilyn
My daughter

Your love for women from many cultures
and countries continues to challenge me.
Thank you for encouraging me to write this book.

Contents

Foreword
A Legacy of Faithful, Tender Light

Rachel Pieh Jones

I met Polly through these pages and through her delightful daughter, Marilyn. This book is Polly's legacy, a gift of memory and relationship, passing along the scents and tastes, sounds, language, and clothing of a life well-lived in Pakistan. But even more important, *in* this book is Polly's legacy–in the lives of the women who loved her, and the women she loved. As Christians, we are not our own. We belong to a loving God. But also, we belong to humanity, to each other. Our lives are stories of a complex and unique tapestry. All those we have loved, lost, held, and celebrated woven together to form us into who are meant to be. Polly's legacy of love shines through the stories of her interactions with these women and their families and lives on and on, down the generations.

Polly loved Jesus, that is so evident in these pages. She loved her family. She loved her Pakistani community. She was faithful to these three loves for more than thirty years living in Pakistan, and her faithfulness continues. She gave herself to relationship and to her Lord with joyful faithfulness. My generation is hungry, I believe, for stories of those who have gone before us and have fought the good fight, kept the faith, finished the race well. This is a story of that kind, a story of hard, joyful, satisfying faithfulness.

Polly, as a white American Christian, couldn't have been more different from the women she met in Pakistan. In these pages I first saw Polly's tenderness toward the delights and fears of the women she encountered. But then I realized the tenderness was also for Polly, from the women who recognized the outsider in their midst and welcomed her, different religious convictions, cultural variances, and all. And then, ultimately, in these stories I see a tender love from God, who saw them all – a foreigner desperate for community, for language help, for cultural guidance, for spiritual connection, and Pakistani women in need of work, friendship, relationship. God saw them and brought them together.

This is a book of hope. In 2020, in a world divided by race, religion, and class, I am eager for stories of light. In Jan Richardson's words in *Circle of Grace*, I see Polly's legacy of faithful, tender light.

Blessed Are You Who Bear the Light
(excerpt)

> *Blessed are you*
> *in whom*
> *the light lives,*
> *in whom the brightness blazes—*
> *your heart*
> *a chapel,*
> *an altar where*
> *in the deepest night*
> *can be seen*
> *the fire that*
> *shines forth in you*
> *in unaccountable faith,*
> *in stubborn hope,*
> *in love that illumines*
> *every broken thing*
> *it finds.*

Introduction

$\mathcal{M}$y husband Ralph and I began our life in Pakistan in the fall of 1954. We returned to the USA to retire in December 1988. During those years we lived in a small town and four different cities in the Sindh Province in Southern Pakistan. We arrived knowing little about Pakistan or its culture, and not a word of Sindhi, the regional language, or Urdu, the national language. With hard work and many mistakes along the way, we learned to communicate in both languages and to feel at home with Pakistanis. Some of our friends were poor and illiterate, others were wealthy and highly educated, and many were part of Pakistan's growing middle class. Among them were Christians from different backgrounds as well as many Muslims and a small number of Hindus. We learned to take off our shoes at the door, and to sit comfortably on a mat or carpet on the floor or on a *charpai,* a rope-strung bed, with our feet tucked under us. Occasionally we might be ushered to a place on a chair or a sofa.

Pakistan is not a culture in which first names are casually used. It is vital to know the proper way to greet a person. Children, teenagers, and younger women called me

Auntie. As a foreigner I was sometimes called *"Memsahib."* *Sahib* meaning Sir was used for foreign men and *Memsahib* for their wives. This title faded from use after Pakistan's independence, except in the case of servants. Upper class Pakistani women were often addressed as *"Begum Sahiba."*

But most often I was called sister. *Bhaji* in Urdu or *Bhairn* in Sindhi soon found their way into my vocabulary. Sometimes this was purely courtesy, a polite way to greet this foreign woman. But in some friendships, forged over many years, sister came to mean something more. This book is about those friends who became sisters to me. None of the friendships described in this book occurred in my early years in Pakistan. Although we lived in the small town of Ratodero for seven years, I cannot point to a single lasting relationship from that time. Those were busy years of learning Sindhi and the culture of the people around us. Four of our five children were born during that time, and I was learning how to make a home for my family with few conveniences in a land that was strange to me. I met many women and can look back on numerous conversations and cups of tea in my home or theirs. But I was too new, too foreign, too busy with my small children, to become a real sister to any of those women.

God continued to call us back to Pakistan, though I often returned reluctantly, imagining an easier life in America. And it was only after many years that some of my friends became true sisters. Among the sisters I describe here, some are Muslims and some are Christians. My desire for each of you who read these chapters is that you will look around in your town, city, workplace, and neighborhood to see immigrants who will become your sisters. May the Lord, who loves people from every nation, open your eyes and your heart to love the strangers among us.

I have changed the names of many of these women to protect the privacy of those who are still alive as well as those who have passed on. To refresh my memory, I have referred to my many journals as well as letters written to my mother and others. In some instances I have relied mainly on my memory, trusting that these recollections are in the main true to the original happenings. I have reconstructed conversations at times, but I have also found that I recorded many conversations in my journals. In some of these stories, where I am familiar with the back story, I have included it to help you understand this woman better. You will learn that with many of them, I was only one person out of many used by God in the woman's life. What a privilege for me to have entered so deeply into the lives of these precious sisters!

1

Mai
My Servant, My Sister

*M*ai dragged herself into the kitchen a half hour late. She looked terrible, and her cough was worse. I put my hand on her forehead. She was burning with fever.

"Oh, Mai," I said, "you're really sick, aren't you. Here, sit down. Let me make you some tea and some toast and we'll talk about it."

I left the kitchen and came back with my Sindhi New Testament. I would send her to the Christian Hospital on a tonga, the horse and buggy we used for a taxi, but first we would have tea. I briefly thought of just sending her home. I needed help, and she was not going to be much use to me at least for some weeks. But by then I had learned her story.

*M*ai had appeared at our front door a few months before. We had just returned from the US, and I was struggling to make a home out of a sprawling bungalow located on the outskirts of the city. Our mission wanted us to live in Shikarpur and had rented this large and unusual building from the Holland Eye Hospital. The Eye Hospital had been forced to discontinue their annual winter eye camps in Shikarpur, so they would not be using the bungalow for the time being. From the front the building looked like a motel, with a center section and two wings of bedrooms. Also like a motel, the Holland bungalow had been built to accommodate a large number of people, including the senior staff of Quetta Mission Hospital and visiting eye surgeons from England or North America. The house was too big for one family, and we were remodeling to accommodate our co-workers, Paul and Mary Pegors, on one side. Even half of it was still quite large, with the veranda running across the whole front of the house. Each bedroom opened onto that veranda. I was finding it a challenge to make this place feel like home.

With all the work going on, everything was filthy, covered with the dust of renovations as well as the normal dust from the desert. I needed some help in the house. I hoped to get a Christian helper, and anticipated that someone in the Christian colony who needed extra money would surely be interested. I had not found anyone when Iqbal, an employee of Shikarpur Christian Hospital, brought Mai to my door.

"Memsahib," he said. "I heard that you were looking for a woman to help you in the house, and this lady needs some work. Her name is Mai Bhaiti, but you can call her Mai."

I looked doubtfully at this tiny lady. Did she weigh even 80 pounds? She was less than five feet tall, and her plain cotton clothes hung on her thin frame. Her gray hair was tied back in a bun with a few curls escaping around her brown and wrinkled face. Her eyes were bright and her mouth looked ready to smile. We were standing on the veranda outside the living room. I motioned to a chair and invited Mai to sit down. I said goodbye to Iqbal, thanking him for thinking of us, but I had huge doubts. Mai was a Muslim. I wanted a Christian woman to help me. I wondered if she could manage the light work I needed done. As if she read my mind, Mai began to tell me how strong she was. "I can do whatever you need me to do," she insisted.

My doubts grew. Would she really be able to walk to our house every day, much less keep up with the workload?

I asked about her family. Where did she live? Mai had one son. He had two wives and seven children. His second wife was pregnant, and he had no job. Her oldest grandson was grown and married, and his wife was expecting a baby. He didn't have a job either. They all lived together in a small house and currently had no income. What about her husband?

"Oh," she answered with a toss of her head, "he threw me away and went off to Karachi to find a younger woman."

In the end, I reluctantly hired her. "I only need you for half the day," I said, "from 7:30 until after lunch. You will need to wash dishes and cook our lunch. I need you to do some of the cleaning, but I understand that you don't do the floors or clean the bathrooms. In December when my children come from school, there will be more cooking, washing clothes and other work."

She assured me that the work was no problem, and she could do everything I needed. Mai was a Sindhi, and this turned out to be a greater help than I anticipated. After being away from Pakistan for two years, having a Sindhi woman in my house, speaking Sindhi with me every day, was an immense benefit. And Mai was a talker.

I soon found that she smoked the little brown cigarettes that were such a curse in this country. They were cheap and easily available to poor people. I chided her for this bad habit and told her in no uncertain terms that she must not smoke in the kitchen.

"No, no!" she assured me. "I promise, I will only smoke outside."

She had a cough, and I wondered about tuberculosis. No, I didn't want to think of that possibility. It must be the smoking and the constant dust from the repairs that were still going on.

Mai had only been working for us a few weeks when she came into the kitchen seriously ill. I was sure now that she had TB. What was I to do? I knew one thing. If I just fired her, she would go home and lie down and die. In that process how many more in her house would be infected? No, I couldn't do it. How would I live with myself?

While Mai drank the tea and ate the toast, I opened the New Testament to Matthew 11:28. Before I read, I told her, "Mai, you are quite sick, and I'm sending you to the Christian hospital with a note for Dr. Mary. I can't cure you, and I don't know what the doctor will say. I also know your family's problems. I don't have jobs for your son or your grandson. But I do know someone who can do all things. *Isa Masih*, Jesus Christ. He is the Son of God, He cares, and He hears us when we pray. Here is what He says in the *Injil*, the Gospel: 'Come to me all you who are weary and burdened, and I will give you rest. Take my yoke upon you and learn from me and you will find rest for your souls.' "

I prayed for Mai that day, for God to hear our prayer in the name of Jesus, for healing, for provision of jobs for her son and grandson. I felt very helpless, but I put it all onto the Lord. This was far more than I could handle on my own.

Mai returned from the hospital later the same day with a note from Dr. Mary, informing me that Mai did indeed have TB. Mary had given her enough medicine for a month and an appointment to come back. She could continue working after the fever went down, in about a week. But she should not handle dishes or food for three months. The note concluded, "If you can help her to have a better diet, she will recover. I've also spoken strongly to her about her smoking."

Mai told me, "Dr. Sahiba says I can keep smoking and die. If I stop, I might live, if God wills."

"Well, what will you do?" I was skeptical.

"Oh, I've already thrown my cigarettes away. I want to live!" Miserable as she was, she smiled at me. "You wanted me to stop, didn't you?"

In spite of her tiny frame and this terrible disease, Mai was strong. She faithfully took her medicine. After the first week she came back to work. I told her that she could eat breakfast and lunch in the kitchen. I wanted her to have an egg and fruit every day and I told her she could cook her lunch using our spices and whatever we had on hand. I gave her dishes with instructions to keep them separate from ours. I explained that she should do the same at home so that her little grandchildren wouldn't get TB.

After she was pronounced safe to cook and wash dishes, she prepared lentils, vegetable or meat curries, with *chapati,* at lunch time, for herself and us. Once a week, if we found fresh fish, she fixed a fish curry, better than any we had eaten in a restaurant. And she began to put on weight. After only a few months, she was quite chubby!

After I read to Mai from the Gospel that first time, we continued reading, beginning with Jesus' birth in Matthew, and I prayed with her each day. If I happened to be busy at my desk, forgetting to read with her, she would come looking for me.

"Oh, Memsahib, you forgot to read with me today," she gently rebuked me. How could whatever I was doing at my desk be more important than our Bible reading and prayer?

As we spent time together in the kitchen, Mai wanted to know all about our family. I told her about my widowed mother, and our two sons, Ed and Tom, now living in America. Marilyn and Dan were studying in boarding school in the far northern mountains in Murree. Our son Stan, and Paul Johnson, his friend from Murree Christian School, had traveled through Europe on their way to Pakistan in an old Land Rover purchased in England. A serious road accident in Turkey interrupted their journey. Both boys had head injuries requiring a hospital stay and an extensive time of recovery in Ankara. This had derailed their plans to spend the year working at Murree Christian School. Mai was overjoyed and pronounced a loud blessing over Stan when she met him on his arrival in Pakistan. He completed his recovery with us over the next few months.

Friday was Mai's day off, and one Thursday after lunch dishes were done and the kitchen cleaned up, she asked me if she could have a copy of the book we were reading to take home.

"But you don't read, Mai. What will you do with it?" I asked her.

"My grandchildren can read. They go to school. They can read it to me tomorrow when I don't come to you." She went off carrying her own copy of the New Testament, wrapped carefully in a cloth I gave her for that purpose.

A few weeks later Mai asked me for another copy of the *Injil*.

"What happened to the one I gave you?" I asked.

"Oh, a relative was visiting and he started to read it. He liked it so I gave it to him." She shrugged as if to say, "How could I refuse?"

So I gave her another copy. After this happened several more times, I shook my head, thinking about this tiny illiterate Muslim Sindhi woman giving away copies of the New Testament to her Muslim relatives. God really does have a sense of humor.

One day as I sat drinking tea with Mai, I wondered aloud how old she was. She didn't know the date of her birth, but she remembered being about twelve or thirteen at the beginning of "the Great War," meaning World War Two. She had married young but learned to be a birth attendant from an older auntie. She told me about being invited to learn more about delivering babies from British nurses who were working in the local Civil Hospital when Pakistan was still a part of India and a British colony. When I shared this with Dr. Mary, she was intrigued by Mai's midwifery experience. One day after a routine check up at the mission hospital, she asked Mai about it. Mai had apparently learned well because she told Dr. Mary all she had been taught about cleanliness during the delivery process. These unknown women had carefully taught her how a midwife could know when the baby could not be safely delivered. At that point it was very important to get the woman to a hospital and a doctor who could help her.

Mai was about my age, according to our estimates, but she considered herself too old to go out at night to deliver babies. For that reason she had come to me and continued to help us for several more years.

$\mathcal{A}$ few months later I stood in my kitchen on a busy Friday. Winters in Sindh are cool enough for a sweater in the daytime, and the nights are chilly, although the temperatures almost never drop to freezing. I loved this cool season when our children came home from boarding school for their long three month holiday. Marilyn and Dan had spent the last nine months 800 miles north in the mountains at Murree Christian School. Mai was happy to meet our two youngest children, and she especially loved Marilyn, our teenage daughter. Stan was still recovering, and we were glad to have this time with him. We had a busy, lively household.

I was feeling especially pressed that Friday morning. A group of young world travelers passing through Shikarpur had experienced car trouble. Not many of the local people spoke enough English to communicate with such travelers. A kind Pakistani had sent them to us. They spent the night in our home, and after breakfast Ralph took them out to get their vehicle repaired so they could get on their way. After my three kids had done the breakfast dishes, the boys disappeared outside to work on a hot air balloon they had designed. As I was trying to plan dinner as well as lunch for my crowd of hungry young people, I heard the front door open and looked up. From where I stood in the kitchen, I could see straight through the large dining room and the living room to the screened veranda at the front of the house. Tim Johnson, a blond teenager, was coming through the living room toward the back of the house.

"Hi, Auntie Polly. My mom needs a recipe. She sent a note. I need to get back as soon as you can copy it for her. I'll be out front with Stan and Dan. Call me when it's ready."

Tim turned around and headed back outside, preferring to spend what time he had with my boys.

"Oh my, what else?" I thought. I read Connie's note, and reached for my cookbook. Only a recipe for a vanilla pudding with eggs. In America Connie would have a package on the shelf, or she could phone me. Here we had to do just about everything from scratch. Nothing was instant, and when someone needed anything, we just stopped to help.

As I copied the recipe, I heard another voice calling me, this time speaking in Sindhi. I looked up to see Mai coming in. She didn't usually come on Fridays. Why was she here? And what was she carrying? She came in with a big smile on her wrinkled, brown face, a newspaper wrapped bundle in her hands, and greeted me, "How are you today, and is everyone well?"

I returned the greeting and asked about her family. As she opened the package in her hands, I could smell it before I saw what she had brought.

"I know how much you like this kind of fish, and when the fish *walla* came by my house, I ran out to get it for you."

At first I didn't know whether to laugh or cry. This day was getting just too confused. What was I to do with this huge fish, still with its head, tail and innards attached? But I had to appreciate her thoughtfulness, especially since she had walked all the way from her home to bring it to me. I looked at the fish, and realized I was seeing our dinner. This fish was huge, big enough to feed my dinner crowd.

"Well, Mai, this is really a very nice fish, and I will get the money to pay for it. But the problem is, who is going to clean it?"

Fresh fish in our small city came from the fish man who goes through the streets selling it from door to door. It is always fresh, caught that morning in the canal or the Indus River at Sukkur, 35 miles away. Pakistanis want to see the whole fish, since that must be proof it was only a very short time ago swimming in the river.

I said to her, "It's your day off, Mai, but I guess you will have to stay long enough to clean and cut up the fish. I'll bake it in the oven for dinner."

I looked at this tiny lady, still small but with more flesh on her bones than when I first met her. I smiled, and she smiled back at me. "Oh, that's no problem," she said cheerfully, as she opened a drawer to find a knife. She took a cutting board from the cupboard, and went out the back door to squat down and clean the fish on the back doorstep.

Mai had become a part of the family.

After two years living in the Holland Bungalow, we moved to a house near Mai's home. With a shorter walk to work and no more smoking, her health was now quite robust. I continued to read with Mai every day. If I forgot, she reminded me. Easter was coming and I was reading the account of Christ's death from Matthew's gospel. As I read of His crucifixion, I looked up. Tears were streaming down her face.

"What is it, Mai? Are you all right?" I asked her.

She looked at me through her tears, and putting her hands on her head, she said, "Oh, now I understand. *Isa Masih* took my sins on His head when He died."

I sat for a few seconds, amazed. But why? This was the power of the Word of God and yes, of prayer. I had prayed for Mai, but I had hardly dared to believe that God would really open the heart of this Muslim woman.

We talked about God's love, Jesus' sacrifice on the cross to save us from the guilt and punishment we deserve. I couldn't wait for Easter so I turned the page to read the Gospel account of what happened on that third day. Mai really understood, believing with all her heart, that Jesus died on that cross for her, to save her from her sins. I had often emphasized to her that Jesus is not a dead prophet like the dead saints whose tombs Sindhis visit to get healing or answers to their prayers. Yes, He died, but God raised Him from the tomb on the third day, and He is alive in heaven. For the first time that day after I prayed, Mai prayed in the name of Jesus, thanking Him for his death on the cross to save her from her sins. Sometime later Mai told me that whenever she heard the call to prayer from the Mosque, especially the early morning *Azan*, she prayed in Jesus' name.

Around that time I had begun writing a Sindhi grammar for newcomers to Sindh. We had never had an adequate course for learning the language. We expected a number of new people from Canada, and we needed to give them something better than the patchwork Sindhi course we had managed to learn from. Anne, a young single woman, was the first to arrive. She lived with us during her first several months in Shikarpur. She and her teacher, a young woman who was a college drop-out, were the first to use the lessons I was preparing. I managed to keep one lesson ahead of them, and was continually revising as they made suggestions. Mai turned out to be a great resource as I struggled to put together this grammar. I was not a linguist, but I loved the Sindhi language and the Sindhi women I had learned to communicate with. I didn't want this grammar book to be a scholarly treatise, rather something practical that would help people to speak the way ordinary Sindhis spoke. They shouldn't sound like a book. Whenever I had a question, Mai was right there in the kitchen. She was a gift to Anne, too, a native Sindhi speaker to talk with as she practiced what she was learning.

Sometimes as I sat working at my manual typewriter, Mai came and squatted at my feet.

"Oh, Memsahib, you must be so tired, sitting there on that hard chair. You are working so hard!"

She could not understand how I could sit on a chair and be comfortable, how I could pound away on the keys of the typewriter most of the morning. By contrast she felt most at ease squatting on the kitchen floor to shell peas or clean rice or lentils. Then she began massaging my feet and legs. I not only had a very competent cook, and a great house helper, I also had a very intelligent language consultant. Illiteracy is an accident of one's place of birth, or economic status, or of being born a girl. It is totally unrelated to intelligence, and Mai was proof of that. Along the way, this small Sindhi woman had become my friend, my sister, my language consultant and even my massage therapist.

*W*hen we moved again to another house further away, Mai decided that she really didn't need to work anymore. Now she was old and her son and grandson both had jobs.

"They can take care of me now," she informed me proudly.

She still visited me quite regularly and I often stopped by her home to catch up on the news of the family and to see her from time to time.

When we went back to the US for a visit, I heard from one of our co-workers that Mai had died. I was so sorry not to be there, but I couldn't feel too sad. Although I would miss Mai terribly, I could imagine her praising Jesus, dancing her way around heaven just as she used to dance around our kitchen at the Holland Bungalow with Marilyn, singing Sindhi folk songs.

2

Ameena
Fearful yet Courageous

*A*meena arrived at my house looking distraught. I led her into the living room, and went to ask Sadorah, my kitchen helper, to make some tea for us.

"What is the trouble, sister?" I asked as I sat down beside her.

"Oh, Memsahib, I'm so sorry but I won't be able to make your clothes any more. I'm too afraid of what might happen to me." She twisted her hands together and looked at me with a sad and fearful expression.

"But why?" I asked. "What are you afraid of?"

"It's the *Jinn,*" she said. "They keep coming to me and telling me if I keep on sewing for the foreigners, they will curse my family and terrible things will happen."

A few months earlier, I had learned about a seamstress in my neighborhood. In the towns and cities where we lived, it was much more comfortable and culturally appropriate to dress as our local friends did. Their fashions involved full pants called *shalwar* with a dress, a *kameez,* over it. A matching *dupatta,* a headscarf, completed the outfit. I wore a headscarf when outside my home or inside if we had guests. I liked the clothes, but the dupatta was hard to get used to, so I seldom wore it at home. The styles were modest and comfortable, but ready-made clothes were not available in the small cities where we lived. I had to go to a cloth shop to buy the material and then find a tailor to sew it up for me. There were men in the bazaar who did tailoring for women. When we had lived in Larkana, my Pakistani Christian friend, Mona, took me to her tailor, and he did a great job. But now we were living in Shikarpur and I had to find someone here to make my clothes. I was delighted to hear about Ameena, a seamstress who lived in my neighborhood.

I sent a message to Ameena's house asking her to come and talk with me about doing some sewing. Ameena was thin, about my height, and unassuming. She was wearing nondescript clothes that certainly didn't advertise her profession. She assured me that if I wasn't satisfied, she would take the outfit apart and do it over till it suited me. She needed the money. Her husband was sick all the time and not able to work. She had three daughters and a young son, all still in school. They lived in a couple of rooms attached to her brother's home. He was younger with a wife and five children. I didn't get the impression that she got much help from him. Ameena apparently was the sole support for her family.

From then on I saw Ameena fairly often, either in my home or hers. I needed a variety of outfits: some for special occasions when I needed to dress up, cotton sets for wearing around the house, lightweight for summer, a bit heavier for the short cool season. I met Ameena's family, a younger sister who taught in a primary school, her brother and his wife, and the children. I wondered why Ameena had never gone to school while her sister Fareeda and two more sisters, also younger, now married, were educated. Ameena seemed to be looked down on, not respected even though she was the older sister. I saw how hard it is to be an illiterate woman in Pakistan with a sick husband and children to support, feed and educate.

Ameena became a part of my life, sometimes coming to my home to get a new sewing job, sometimes just dropping in to chat.

After Ralph and I became better acquainted with the family, we were invited to a circumcision party for Ameena's nephew. We walked from our house to a narrow lane lined with open drains on each side carrying waste water and sewage. I remembered Fareeda, Ameena's younger sister, complaining about the useless politicians who came around to their neighborhood before an election.

"If only you vote for me, I will see that your street is paved and that you have proper drainage. I will do away with these filthy drains." The candidate made lavish promises.

Fareeda, in disgust, had said, "Do they do anything for us? And do we ever see them again? Never, until the next election!"

Arriving at the house, now festooned with colored streamers, I left Ralph outside where the men were gathered and entered the crowded courtyard. The little boy about eight years old was lying on a charpai, a red silk sheet over his small body. According to custom, the circumcision had been performed by a local barber, and now the young lad was enthroned in the midst of his female relatives and family friends. The men had witnessed the cutting; now the women of the family took over to speak their blessings over him and praise him for his bravery.

When a Muslim child is born, the father or grandfather whispers into the baby's ear the Muslim creed, "There is no God but Allah, and Muhammad is his messenger." This ensures that the very first words this Muslim child hears are those of the creed, that most important of all declarations of a Muslim's faith. For a boy the next significant event will be his circumcision, not as an infant, but at the age of six or eight.

As I greeted the women, most dressed in their best silks and satins and adorned in gold jewelry, I looked around for Ameena. I found her in a corner wearing her very ordinary cotton outfit.

"Oh, my dear," I thought, "do you never sew a lovely outfit for yourself? How hard it must be to be always making other women beautiful by your sewing and never yourself."

I settled myself down beside her to chat a bit. How were the children doing? One thing was always on her mind. She had to ensure that her daughters were educated, that each one would have a profession, teaching or, if God should will it, medicine, then a good marriage, according to the will of Allah. And her son?

"Oh," she sighed, "He is so naughty. He skips school and plays with some boys who are not good boys. I'm so worried."

I replied, "You must be. We must pray for him. And may God help you in teaching him the right things."

To myself, I thought, "So many people are strict in bringing up their girls, and then spoil their boys. And they often reap the sad results."

The party culminated in a delicious meal of chicken curry and rice pilau followed by sweet rice, likely catered by the same barber. Barbers in Pakistan are men of many talents. It was very much like a wedding feast. As usual we women waited until the men had eaten their fill, but there was no shortage. No matter how poor a family might be, they would never suffer the shame of running out of food at a celebration like this.

Soon after I had eaten, a message came from outside that whenever I was ready to leave, my husband was waiting to take me home. I expressed my thanks to the women of the family and wrapped my shawl around to cover my head and my body. We were silent on our short walk home by the light of a flashlight; there were no streetlights on that small lane. Our thoughts were of these people we had come to love. It was an honor to be invited to this, primarily a family event. We were able to communicate well in their language, Sindhi. But oh, the great gulf between the Good News of God's love in Jesus and their fear of *Jinn,* of black magic, of the evil eye.

Some time later, Ameena came to my house so distraught about the Jinn who were threatening her, warning her to stay away from foreigners. We talked about these spirits or demons that cause so much fear among Muslims. I knew that people went to great lengths to avoid them and to protect their homes and their children from their evil power. *Mullahs*, religious leaders in the community, prepare leather amulets with Qur'anic verses sewn inside. The rosary containing 99 beads, each representing one of the beautiful names of Allah, can be a protection since people believe that these names are powerful to protect against evil.

My heart went out to Ameena, living as she did in such bondage. We talked a bit longer and then I asked if she would like me to pray in the Name of Jesus.

"Jesus, *Hazrat Isa*, is much more powerful than any jinn." I told her. "When He died on the cross as the sacrifice for our sin and rose from the dead on the third day, He defeated all the power of Satan. He is alive today in heaven at the right hand of God, and He hears us when we pray in His Name."

She wanted me to pray and I did, asking God to reveal Himself to her, to protect her in the Name of Jesus from the power of these jinn who were tormenting her. I asked Him to bless her family and to enable her to continue to do the good work she was doing to support them.

Her demeanor had changed and she seemed to be much more at peace than when she came in. She continued to sew for me and for other missionaries. I continued to pray for her that God in His great love and mercy would open her eyes and her heart and mind to know the truth and freedom she could know in Christ.

After we left Pakistan, I occasionally heard news of Ameena and her family. Her daughters finished high school and entered the Women's College in Shikarpur. They worked part time, teaching Sindhi to some of the women missionaries. The curriculum included Bible reading. In this way they read and heard the Gospel. Rozina became a teacher and, like her aunt Fareeda, remained single. After her son married, Ameena moved out of her brother's house to live in an upstairs apartment in her son's home with Rozina. She arranged marriages for her other two daughters and they were living near her in Shikarpur. A few years ago Ameena suffered a stroke which left her paralyzed on the left side. She had good treatment in a private hospital in the nearby city of Sukkur, and recovered use of her left hand and leg. I am happy to hear good news of my sister, that she and her children are doing well, that they are caring for their mother.

But oh, how my heart longs to hear of a turning to Jesus, and I continue to pray for that good news.

3

Grace
Always Persevering

One winter evening, after an early sunset, I was surprised to see Grace walk into my living room. Had she come alone in the dark across the city from her father's house?

"No," she answered my question. "My brother brought me and he is visiting a friend nearby. I had to see you." She sat down on the sofa and I sat next to her. I asked about tea.

"No, no," Grace began to cry. "I just need to talk. I don't know what to do." Benjamin, her husband, had left her a few months before, and she had moved back to her parents' home.

I listened as she poured out her heart. She was pregnant, three months now.

"Alice says that Bubbly and Sammy are enough of a burden for the household," she told me, "And I should have an abortion."

Grace was part of the Punjabi Christian community in Pakistan that traces its spiritual heritage to a remarkable nineteenth century revival. In 1873 a small, dark-skinned, lame man named Ditt arrived at the home of a Presbyterian missionary asking to be baptized. Samuel Martin felt he should give this illiterate villager from the low caste Chuhra tribe some teaching before baptizing him. But Ditt objected saying he could not stay. He related his story of hearing the Gospel from a former Hindu and putting his faith in Jesus Christ as his Savior from sin. Martin, after talking it over with his wife and praying, could find no biblical reason not to baptize Ditt. After his baptism, Ditt disappeared, returning to his village to share his new faith with his family. Two years later he returned bringing his wife, his daughter and two neighbors whom he had led to faith in Christ. Ditt never learned to read, but spent his life going from village to village preaching, often enduring persecution. During his lifetime thousands from his *Chuhra* tribe left Hinduism and became Christians (Frederick and Margaret Stock, *People Movements in the Punjab*, Pasadena, California: William Carey Library, 1975).

From these roots the Punjabi chuch grew into the largest group of Christians in Pakistan. Many are now educated and work as nurses, doctors, teachers and shopkeepers, but a large number remain illiterate sweepers. They are often discriminated against and find it difficult to rise out of their menial jobs.

Grace's parents, Karam Masih and his wife, were Punjabi Christians from the city of Sahiwal north of Sindh.

Grace was the eldest of their eight children. Her father and mother had committed their lives to Christ. Although uneducated themselves, they were determined to provide their children with a good education. Karam learned to read through an Adult Literacy program begun in their area. As he began to read and study the Bible, he grew into a deep understanding of his faith. This also led him to a deeper commitment of his personal life to Christ.

Grace went to school through eighth grade, and then stayed home to help her mother in the house and with the younger children. Her siblings all finished high school. Her sister, Alice, became a midwife and was offered a position in the Civil Hospital in Larkana, Sindh. The family moved with Alice into the small house on the hospital compound which was allotted to her as a part of her compensation as a hospital employee.

Two of her brothers were employed by the railway, one in a dispensary, the other as a mail clerk, another became an electrician. Her sister Sosan became a nurse, and Shokat and Elizabeth, the youngest, became doctors. The family began to attend Saint Stephen's, the only protestant church in the city. Karam became a leader in the church.

Around that time Benjamin moved to Larkana. He was a Sindhi believer in Jesus and a former Muslim who worked for the the Sindhi Branch of the Pakistan Bible Correspondence School. His widowed mother and only sister had not disowned him when he became a Christian, but he knew he could not expect them to arrange a marriage with a Christian woman. At Saint Stephen's Church he found the woman he wanted to marry, but he could not go directly to her father. He needed someone to act in the place of his parents.

Our co-workers Jack and Edna Christensen were living in Larkana at the time, and it was not unusual for Benjamin to drop in to visit with them. One evening, as they drank tea together, they were taken aback by his request, "Will you be my parents?"

Why was this twenty-something young man asking them to adopt him? Benjamin explained his dilemma. He wanted to marry Grace, Karam Masih's daughter. In the place of his own parents, he needed someone to take his request to her father, to intercede for him. Would Jack and Edna be willing? After spending time praying and pondering the implications of stepping into the place of parents for this Christian brother, the couple approached Karam and his wife to ask them to consider giving his daughter to Benjamin in marriage.

For Grace's father this was not a decision to be taken lightly. As a Pakistani father he carried a heavy responsibility for Grace's future. Marriage in Pakistan is not a matter of two people falling in love and deciding to marry. It is much more a matter of two families coming together through the arranging of a marriage. Ideally the church should become a new family for a believer from a Muslim background. But these situations are seldom ideal. Christians have a very hard time trusting the sincerity of a new Christian. Often when facing difficulties in this new life, the convert returns to Islam. Local Christians had heard of this happening. But Benjamin had been a Christian for some years and had remained faithful. He appeared to be accepted by the Christians in Larkana. After prayer and consulting his wife, their adult sons and Grace, Karam accepted the proposal. Grace and Benjamin were married in 1964.

Benjamin and Grace seemed happy. A baby girl was born to them and they named her Shazia. As she grew into a healthy, happy child, they gave her the nickname Bubbly. When a new couple, Ben and Betty Ralston came to Larkana to study Urdu, Betty developed a deep friendship with Grace. Even though she felt limited in her ability to communicate in Urdu, Betty studied the Bible with Grace in preparation for her baptism. At the time she wrote, "What love–Christ's love–has been planted in our hearts for one another."

But Benjamin became increasingly discontent in his work at the Bible Correspondence School. When Grace gave birth to a son, both parents were overjoyed, but the baby failed to thrive. When the child died, Benjamin became so distraught that he was unable even to make arrangements for the burial and graveside service. Then the couple moved away from Larkana for a period of time, and Benjamin went through a period of deep spiritual struggle. Grace returned to her family in Larkana. Even with all the heartache, she remained a loyal and loving wife. During all this time, the responsibility of caring for Grace and her children fell to Karam Masih. Her family never let them suffer material need.

*M*y friendship with Grace began when we moved to Larkana. As I became acquainted with this young woman, her sweet spirit impressed me. True to her name she was filled with grace. Her faith and trust in the Lord never wavered. At the time she and the children were staying with her family. After Benjamin returned, the couple continued to live with Karam's family for some time. However, since he seemed to be more settled and had returned to church, Karam allowed Benjamin to move the family into a small house near the church and close to our home. This gave me more opportunity to spend time with Grace. One day I stepped through the door of her courtyard to see her turning over bricks and resetting them.

She explained to me, "They are old and worn so I am turning them all over to use the bottom side. See over there where I have finished and cleaned them."

I looked over toward the wall as she pointed. I don't think I would ever have considered doing such a thing, but the finished corner looked like new.

She laid the bricks in her hand into place and stood. "Come," she said, "I can stop and we will have some tea."

We went into the veranda where she had a small kitchen with a gas stove. She brought a chair for me and we chatted. I asked about Benjamin and about the children. Bubbly was in school, and Sammy in a pre-school. Her husband had gone to Sukkur for the day and she expected him back before dark.

"There is a possibility of a job," she smiled, "but we will stay here and he will go by bus each day."

We drank tea together, Grace got her Bible and showed me something she had a question about. We talked for some time, and then we prayed together. I left, urging her to come across to my house any time.

"And you know you can bring the children. They like to play in the yard and the Pastor's children always like to play with them, too." Our local Pastor and his family lived on the other side of our yard. I hugged her as I left, thanking the Lord for this precious sister.

Benjamin never returned home that night, nor the next day. Grace discovered that he had even taken some of her wedding jewelry, probably to sell it. To steal his wife's wedding jewelry is something no decent husband would ever do in Pakistan. It is the one thing along with her clothes that belongs strictly to her alone.

Grace didn't live in that little house long enough to enjoy the clean new courtyard she had worked so hard for. After waiting a few days, she moved back with her children to her father's house. I continued to see her, and she came occasionally to my house. We prayed and sometimes cried together. She was such a lovely woman. What was Benjamin thinking to walk away from his marriage, his children whom he seemed to love?

*N*ot long after, Grace came to tell me she was pregnant. The majority of Pakistanis, including Christians, believe that a baby in the womb is not really a person until the baby takes its first breath. Grace didn't want to abort her baby, but until she came to me she had only told her sister Alice. Her parents didn't know about the pregnancy, although she thought her mother might suspect.

As I listened, I was praying hard. How could I advise Grace? She was heartbroken over Benjamin's departure. She had been so happy the few months after he came back. I knew that I could not tell Grace what to do. This had to be her decision. We talked about what God would want her to do. Could she trust God? She knew she could trust her father. He loved his grandchildren so much. His disappointment in Benjamin did not affect his treatment of his daughter or her children. We read a Psalm together and we prayed. We talked about how every life is a gift from God. When Grace left that evening, I wasn't sure what her decision would be, but I learned later that she told her sister that she could not go through with an abortion. She had to trust God and her parents were willing to trust Him, too.

Before the baby's birth, Benjamin returned. He claimed to have repented of his sin, and he asked forgiveness of Grace's parents. He had met with some Swedish Pentecostal missionaries in Karachi and they were willing to give him some work and a place to live. Grace stayed with her parents until after the birth of another son. When the baby was a few months old, Benjamin came back to move his family to Karachi.

We visited them in their new home in Karachi before leaving for the USA for our home assignment. We learned that the Swedish missionaries were in the process of helping the family emigrate to Sweden. When this was finalized, Grace and Benjamin left Pakistan. While we heard news of them from time to time, it was several years before I saw Grace again. She came back to Pakistan with her daughter Shazia to visit her family. Shazia was married with a child and was on an extended paid maternity leave from her job. The boys were doing well. And Benjamin? He was active in the church and working at a good job.

Betty Ralston continued to correspond with Grace. Some years later she called me with the news that Benjamin had become extremely depressed, and had taken his own life.

We were left with so many questions and no answers. Benjamin's spiritual struggles as a believer in Jesus from a Muslim background were intense. We understood this, perhaps as much as anyone who has not faced this kind of spiritual conflict personally. Was his depression in part at least related to that struggle? Ralph had been the first to mentor and disciple Benjamin when he came to work at the Bible Correspondence School as a young man. He had been a part of our family. Our children called him Uncle Benjie. We had prayed for Benjamin and Grace, for their marriage. Other co-workers and Pakistani Christians, including another former Muslim, had mentored and encouraged him. Where had we failed? Was there more that we could have done?

Yet my sister Grace, without knowing the answers to these questions, remained a woman of faith, strong and courageous in her trust in God.

4

Shareefa
Secret Sister

*J*acob, our cook, came in from answering the doorbell and handed me a note.

"So who is this from?" I asked in Urdu.

Jacob was a small man, not much taller than I. He wore glasses and was balding a bit. We hired him as a cook when we moved into this house in the city of Larkana in 1970. He had worked for the Webster family and before that for two other missionary families. Jacob was a Christian and scrupulously honest. He kept a little notebook to record every *paisa* he spent when he shopped for us in the bazaar.

Jacob replied, "Two little girls brought this note, Memsahib, but they didn't want to come in to give it to you. They told me their mother sent it, and then went back home."

I thanked Jacob and he went back to the kitchen. I unfolded the note to read a message written in English on lined paper, "Mrs. Brown, I greet you and hope that you and family are all well. I am Mrs. Nadeem Mohd. I was friend to Mrs. Webster when she used to live here. I want to know you also. Please come to my house. I am writing my address for you. It is not far from your house. *Inshallah,* if God wills, we will meet soon."

I looked at the address she had written. I couldn't possibly find her house in the maze of narrow streets that made up the neighborhoods around us. Street signs were a rarity in the city of Larkana. Perhaps Jacob could help. I went out to the kitchen to talk this over with him. We had found it helpful in so many ways to have a local man, a Christian helper in our home.

"I know about them," he said. "Her husband has a shop, but I don't know where they live. She should send one of the children to take you there."

He paused, thinking, then added, "I think sister Mona might know her. When I go home I'll ask her."

Mona was one of the Christian women who lived in a small house in the compound surrounding the church. She worked as a midwife doing home deliveries all over the city. She very likely knew this family.

The next week, after making arrangements through notes sent back and forth, I was walking through the narrow streets toward Shareefa's house. She had sent her older daughter Parveen, a pretty child, to show me the way. I had learned Shareefa's first name from Mona who had delivered her children. The little girl, perhaps 10 years old, walked demurely by my side. She wore a print dress over her *shalwar,* the full pants worn by women and girls in Pakistan. How did the child manage her *dupatta,* her head scarf, so gracefully? I envied these little Pakistani girls.

48

The dupatta was the one thing I had not learned to like in wearing Pakistani clothes. It was always slipping and sliding and I found myself constantly adjusting it to keep it from falling off my head. Of course, Parveen had probably begun wearing one at the age of five when she started school. Like the language, and making *chapatis,* the local flatbread, some things are just easier to learn as a child from one's mother. I looked down at Parveen and asked her about school. She was in fourth class and today school was closed for some reason. She didn't know why, but she liked having a holiday. She smiled up at me as we turned into her street. I had been noting landmarks all the way so I could find my way home. We stepped into a tiny hallway and she pointed to the stairs.

"Our house is upstairs. Ami is waiting. She will be happy to see you," she said as she led me up to the landing and the door at the top of the stairs.

Shareefa, probably in her thirties, rose from the sofa to greet me with an embrace. She took my shawl and hung it on a hook by the door. It would be some time before we were on a first name basis. In Pakistan I knew many women as "sister" for a long time before knowing them by name. This was a middle-class family judging by the sofa set and the carpet on the floor. I had slipped out of my sandals and left them by the door, just as Parveen had done. Shareefa was barefoot and dressed in a cool-looking cotton outfit since the weather was still quite warm. We sat together on the sofa and Parveen disappeared into a side room.

As a foreigner I was often awarded a higher status than I perhaps deserved. I had taken a long time to understand these social cues and I made a lot of mistakes along the way. Pakistani women meeting for the first time were somehow able to judge the social relationship quite easily: Is she my equal, my superior or below me on the social scale? In Pakistani culture it was important to understand this. I now had the advantage of being middle aged with a few gray hairs and teen-aged sons. My age had gained me a measure of respect I had not experienced as a younger woman.

During that first visit we chatted in quite general ways. This was typical in Pakistan, especially when meeting a Muslim woman. I told her this was my second time living in Larkana. The first time I had only just arrived from America and knew no Sindhi or Urdu. I had not met many women and only lived here for a few months before going to Murree for the hot weather and to study the language. I told her about my children away in Murree in boarding school and about my widowed mother in America. I learned that her husband was a shopkeeper and they had moved to Larkana soon after their marriage. She had three children, two daughters and a younger son, all born in Larkana. I had begun speaking in English since we had written our notes in that language. But I soon found that while she could read and write English, she was much more comfortable conversing in Urdu. After we talked for some time, Shareefa offered me tea.

I objected, "Oh, no. You don't need to take any trouble."

Courtesy demanded that I refuse a time or two even as she urged me on, finally getting up and saying, "Of course, you must have some tea before you go home."

She called Parveen and her other daughter, Soraya to sit with me and keep me entertained while she fixed the tea. Their small brother came in with them from the other room where they had been playing.

Shareefa returned carrying a tray with a teapot, cups and a plate of small cookies. The children stayed and had tea and biscuits with us, pouring the hot milky tea into their saucers to cool it, then sipping it from the saucers.

I smiled and told them that my children used to drink their tea that way but now they have grown big and drink it from the cup. A half hour later I had said my goodbyes and was walking back through the narrow streets. The girls had offered to lead me home but I assured them that I could find the way by myself.

Shareefa told me to please come often to her house, and I in turn invited her to come to see me.

"It's really quite close," I reminded her, "it's the same house the Websters lived in. You don't have to go on the main street to get there. You can come in the side door."

She nodded and assured me that she knew the way since she had visited her friend Shirley there several times.

Through the next months and years I saw Shareefa many times, and our friendship deepened. But there always seemed to be something between us. We talked about our families, the rising prices of meat and vegetables, problems of the world and Pakistan. The time never seemed right for me to speak about my faith or to pray with her. Then one day she sent a message saying she needed to see me urgently. I dropped what I was doing and wrapping my *chadder*, my shawl, around me I headed out the side door and down the street toward her house. She was very sick and from the symptoms she described, she needed to see a doctor. I suggested she might go to Shikarpur to the Christian Hospital where there were women doctors.

"But I don't know anyone there," Shareefa objected. "There is a Women's Christian Hospital in Multan where my sister lives. Do you know those doctors? Can you write me a letter of introduction so they will see me?"

"I do know them, and you really don't need a letter to be seen. But if you want me to, I can write one," I replied.

"I will go on the evening train," she said. "I can stop by your house and get the letter. It's on the way to the station."

Shareefa came and got my letter. I asked if I could pray for her in Jesus' Name, and she allowed me to pray. She also took a Christian book to read on the train journey.

Shareefa received treatment at the hospital in Multan and returned feeling much better. After I heard she was back I went over to hear all about her experience. She ushered me into her sitting room as usual.

But I was not prepared for what happened next. The girls were in school and her son was napping in the bedroom. Before sitting down she turned and reached up to a high shelf, taking down a large book wrapped in colorful cloth.

"What is this?" I wondered. "Is she going to read something to me from the Qur'an?" I had noticed this book before but it was not unusual to see a cloth wrapped Qur'an up on a shelf. I pulled my dupatta back over my head from where I had let it slide to my shoulders. I had learned to do this whenever I was with a Muslim friend and we heard the call to prayer. I also did this when I read the Bible with any woman, Muslim or Christian. This was a way of showing respect. She also adjusted her head scarf as she sat down beside me and began to unwrap the book.

I was totally shocked at what I saw next. The book was not a Qur'an, it was an Urdu Bible!

She looked at me and smiled. "You are surprised, I know. You thought that I am a Muslim. No, I am a Christian. I want to tell you my story."

Shareefa had been born into a Christian home. She had an older sister, the one she had visited in Multan, but no other siblings. When she was in her teens, her father died and soon after, her mother. She did not remember what their sickness was, but it could have been any number of diseases endemic to Pakistan. Her uncle took her into his home and before long he informed her that he had made a marriage arrangement. This did not surprise her, but when he told her that the man was a Muslim friend of his, she could not believe that he would do such a thing to his sister's daughter. She cried and begged him to please tell her it wasn't so. But the only answer she got was that the arrangement was settled and she must accept it.

"You can't know how I prayed. I thought surely God would not let this happen to me," Shareefa paused and was silent for a minute.

I didn't know what to say. I was still trying to get my mind around this new revelation. This sister I had thought to be a Muslim was a Christian.

"I fasted for days and even to my wedding day, begging God to prevent the marriage from happening." She continued, "But God did nothing. I had to accept that I was being married into a Muslim family. This would be my fate."

"Oh, Shareefa. I am so sorry but you never told me. I have thought all along that you were a Muslim." I replied.

She unfolded more of her story. Her husband was a good man, he was kind to her and a good father to the children. He only went to the mosque on the big holidays. He asked only that she would not go to church or tell people she was a Christian. He allowed her to have a Bible and to read it, not only to herself but to the children. He had no close family since his parents had both died. She had been spared living under the authority of a Muslim mother-in-law. And recently her husband had begun to study the Bible through the Bible Correspondence School lessons. She had shared her story with Shirley Webster before the Websters left for America. Sister Mona who lived in the church compound also knew, but Shareefa had asked her not to tell anyone lest trouble come to her husband.

*O*ur friendship grew deeper in the months ahead. In her home or mine we read the Bible and prayed together. Then it was time for us to return to the USA for an extended time. On our return we moved to Shikarpur and I lost contact with Shareefa.   When Connie and Larry Johnson moved to Larkana, they developed a close relationship with the whole family. The two girls accepted Christ and the son was very interested. Nadeem Mohammed, Shareefa's husband, was ready to be baptized, but because of his business and the local Muslim community, he felt it wasn't the right time. Then the family moved to Karachi and again we lost contact, not knowing what had become of them.

Several years later, Ralph and I were in Karachi for business and shopping. Since we were going in separate directions, we agreed to meet at our favorite restaurant for lunch. At about 1:30 we were seated at a table and giving the server our order. We looked up to see a woman approaching from a table across the room. She was wearing a black silk burka, but her face was uncovered. It was Shareefa! Eating lunch here with her son, she had recognized us and they sat down at our table to chat for a few minutes. After their move to Karachi, her husband had openly confessed his faith in Christ. The whole family had been baptized and had joined a local church. Sadly Nadeem Mohammed had died the year before, but Shareefa continued strong in her faith and was living with her son who was now married. We parted after talking for some time, thanking God that He was continuing the good work He had begun in this sister and her family.

5

Rasheeda
Where is my sister?

The house was part of a row of connected houses in this narrow lane in the center of the city. I went up the four steps to the door. A burlap curtain hung in the doorway. This curtain would stop any man not closely related to the women inside. But I was a woman and was free to pass through. I pulled the burlap aside and called out as I stepped in.

"Is anyone home?"

As a young lady turned from the other side of the courtyard, I heard Rasheeda, call out from a room just to the left of the entrance.

"Where is my sister? I hear my sister's voice, send her in to me. I want to see my sister. She has come after such a long time."

At that moment I knew why I was here.

*P*akistan was not where I wanted to be that August. The Sindh Province was unbearably hot, the city of Shikarpur a dusty, overgrown village. Our children and our grandchildren were in America. My mother was getting older. Couldn't the Lord find some way to use us there? I knew God had quite clearly shown us that this was where He wanted us, and I had been trying to put my negative thoughts out of my head without much success.

I climbed down from the rear seat of the *tonga,* the horse and buggy conveyance we used as a taxi. The tonga had picked me up at my house on the opposite side of the city. We had come down a main road and through one of the large bazaar areas into a maze of lanes to my friend's home. All the way I had not seen a woman in the streets. In spite of the heat I was wrapped in a large shawl, a *chadder.* It covered me from my head to below my knees. I didn't cover my face though. That covering was worn by Muslims, not Christians. I paid the fare and the gray-haired driver assured me he would return at one o'clock to take me home.

Then I passed through the burlap curtain and heard Rasheeda call out, "Where is my sister?" and I knew why we had returned to Pakistan that August, and why we had kept coming back so many times before. I was accustomed to being called "sister", but this was different. Rasheeda was eager to see me. Over the time I had known her our relationship had deepened. Though Rasheeda was a devout Muslim, and I was a Christian, our friendship had truly made us sisters.

Laila, Rasheeda's daughter, greeted me warmly with a hug and sent me into the room where her mother waited.

"Go in, Auntie," she said, "You can tell Ami is eager to see you."

I stepped into a typical room simply furnished with a *charpai,* a rope bed, covered with a red patterned Sindhi *ajrak,* the traditional tie dyed cloth found in every Sindhi home. It is used for sheets, as a shawl for men or women, and for numerous other purposes. My friend sat on the bed with her legs crossed under her. In front of her a Qur'an sat open on a wooden stand. She called her daughter to come and put the book and stand away. I watched as first Rasheeda then Laila, kissed the Qur'an. Laila carefully wrapped it in a silk cloth and placed it on a high shelf across the room. Then Rasheeda invited me to join her sitting on the bed.

"I haven't seen you for so long. Come, be comfortable, sit here on the bed, " she patted the space beside her. "I want to hear all about your travels to America. How is your mother, your children?"

We exchanged the customary small talk, about health and family and the family's health. Ralph and I had gone to America for our daughter's wedding, and I took pictures out of my bag to show her. She told me about her summer trip to the Shia holy places in Iraq. This wasn't like the annual pilgrimage to Mecca in Saudi Arabia, but it had been a very special time for her. Her nephew had taken her, and she had been back home for a few weeks.

Her daughter brought in tea and cookies and we continued our conversation as we drank the steaming chai. I began to ask her about her reading of the Qur'an. I knew she could read Sindhi. She had told me that her father didn't believe in sending girls to school but he wanted her to be educated. A tutor had come to the house to teach her Sindhi reading and writing and the basics of numbers and arithmetic.

"So I could keep household expense accounts," she had told me.

Curious about her grasp of Arabic, I asked, "And how did you learn Arabic? Do you understand what you read?"

"My father believed that a girl should also be able to read the Qur'an. So the wife of the Mullah came to teach me my Arabic letters and how to read our holy book. I understand a little but not very much. "

I asked her about her prayers, "Your health is not so good. Are you able to pray five times a day?"

Rasheeda answered, "I try to. So on my good days, I try to pray an extra time to make up for the times that I am not able to pray."

I looked at my friend, my sister, and my heart went out to her. "My dear sister," I said, "I think that you have done everything that a human being can do to try to please God!"

"Oh, but I'm such a sinner!" Rasheeda looked truly distressed. "How can such a sinful woman as I am ever do enough to please God?"

"Of course," I answered. "That is so true! No one can be good enough because God is holy. I am a terrible sinner, too, but sister, this is exactly why God sent Jesus into the world. This is the reason He died on the cross. Because He lived a perfect life without ever sinning, His life became a perfect sacrifice for the sins of everyone in the world."

We talked longer, and she acknowledged again her need for forgiveness.

Oh, if she could only go a step further and recognize Jesus as the answer to her need!

Before I left, she asked me if I had a Sindhi book to give her. She pointed to the cupboard opposite her bed. From her visits to our hospital and from my visits with her, she had purchased and had read these Christian books. She had a collection of almost all our Sindhi books. I rummaged in my bag to see if I might have a new one for her. I found a small booklet called "Summary of the New Testament" and showed it to her.

"These are words from the *Injil*, the Gospel of Jesus Christ," I said, holding it out to her. "Do you have this one?"

She took the book, kissed it and laid it on the table, "Thank you. I will read this and thank you for coming. Please come again soon."

I visited Rasheeda several more times in the following months. I never knew just how old she was. It is not easy to judge a woman's age in Pakistan. Life is so hard for most women that they look much older than their age. She complained of feeling weak, and I could see that her health was failing. Then on a visit to her daughter, a doctor in the city of Hyderabad, she was diagnosed with chronic Leukemia and treated with blood transfusions. She didn't want to move away from Shikarpur to the much larger city in the south. For some time she traveled every few months for the transfusions. She felt much better as a result, but then the family decided that it was best for her to move to Hyderabad to live with the older daughter. She allowed me to pray for her one last time and we parted, both a bit tearful.

About a year later Laila sent a message that her mother had died. She herself had been with her mother, and had returned to Shikarpur after her mother's funeral. I went to the home to offer my condolences and found her quite distraught. I told her how sorry I was, and then we sat in silence for some time.

"How was your mother's passing?" I asked. "Was she in much pain or discomfort?"

Laila wiped away tears with her headscarf. "I don't think she had much pain in her body. But she was so fearful!"

My tears came then, and I hugged Laila as we cried together. I tried to comfort her, but what could I say? I had no assurance that my friend, my sister, Rasheeda had made her peace with God through trusting Jesus. She was such a good woman, she had worked so hard to please Him, but she had found Jesus to be a stumbling block.

6
Alice
Suffering yet Rejoicing

$\mathcal{A}$ lice was from the Christian community and worked
as a sweeper, cleaning homes to support her family. She had
been born into a middle class family, and her father had
been a Christian military man. He had died before he could
arrange her marriage. Her mother made an agreement for
her to marry a man named Kishin, a nominal Christian,
and a sweeper.

No formal caste system exists in Pakistan as it does in
India. However, in actual practice there were huge gaps
between social classes. Sweepers are at the bottom, most
of them illiterate and Christians in name only. Their
grandparents had been converted from Hinduism in the
early 1900s during a great movement of people in northwest
India to faith in Christ. They were legally Christians but
unlike their grandparents' generation, most knew little or
nothing about their faith.

Our colleague Mildred Salmon remembered vividly the day Alice came to her house in Jacobabad, squatted at her feet and unburdened her heart.

"Oh, Memsahib," she said, "my children haven't been baptized. I am so afraid they might get sick and die, and then what will happen? They can't go to heaven if they are not baptized. Can your husband baptize them?"

Mildred shared truth from the Bible with Alice that day. No, baptism could not save her children or make them acceptable to God. Faith in Jesus, God's Son, in His death on the cross for our sins is what everyone needs. Alice prayed and received Jesus Christ that day as her Savior. She went home, a new creation in Christ, to share this good news with her children.

Alma Dobra, who had previously lived in Jacobabad, had begun teaching Alice to read through an Adult Literacy program, and Mildred continued this work. She remembered the day Alice struggled word by word through a sentence in her Urdu primer. Suddenly she understood what she had just read!

"Oh, that is from the Bible. I can read the Bible!" Her face shone with joy.

Alice often shared her burdens with Mildred. Her husband was abusive and a compulsive gambler. This was the reason Alice had to work in the lowly job of a sweeper. How else could she earn money to feed her children? When she collected her monthly pay from the people she worked for, she hurried to the bazaar, hoping she would not meet her husband on the way. From her meagre earnings she bought flour, sugar, rice, lentils, tea and other staples so they would have enough to eat during the coming month.

Alice enrolled her children, Jamila and John, in the small Christian school Wil and Mildred started. Her husband objected to the small monthly fee, but she stood firm and paid it promptly every month as soon as she got her pay.

In 1965 when the Salmons returned to the USA for a year long furlough, Ralph and I returned to Pakistan and moved to Jacobabad for a year. Ralph had a working knowledge of Urdu, but I had only studied it for one summer. The two progress tests I had passed only showed me how much I still had to learn. Both of us were fluent in Sindhi, but the Christian community in Jacobabad understood little Sindhi. We needed to speak Urdu to communicate with them.

Following Mildred, who was an excellent Urdu speaker, was a huge challenge for me. I began visiting the various Christians in their homes and I could just about hold my own in conversation. At the end of the first visit when I got up to leave, the women wouldn't let me go.

"Aren't you going to read the Bible and pray with us the way Mrs. Salmon always did?" I had not even brought my Urdu Bible with me. They found a Bible and I managed to find a short passage I could read with their help. I remember stumbling through a prayer and apologizing for my very bad Urdu.

After that experience I prepared for each visit. One day in Alice's home, I took the large print New Literate's New Testament I had brought with me from my bag. Her face brightened. "Oh, I have one like that," and she went to get it. We read together that day and many times after. We often found ourselves helping each other with difficult words. Just two newly literate sisters learning to read Urdu, we often laughed at ourselves as we struggled over a word neither of us recognized.

We only lived in Jacobabad for a year before the Salmons returned. They were far better fitted for that ministry than we were. We moved to the large city of Hyderabad where Ralph facilitated the printing of our Sindhi books. Over the following years I kept in touch with Alice through occasional visits back to Jacobabad. Of all the Christian women I met and visited and prayed with there, Alice is the one I remember as a sister. Her children grew up, and she was able to arrange good marriages for them. John married a girl from Larkana, Soraya, who had been one of "my girls" from the youth group there. Soraya was the daughter of our cook Jacob, and she had grown into a lovely Christian woman with a strong faith. Soon after the birth of their daughter, Soraya was diagnosed with breast cancer. With the limited medical care available for cancer treatment, there was not much hope for her recovery. Not long before she died, her brother in desperation wanted to go to a local *pir*, a Muslim holy man, and get some holy water for her to drink.

Soraya, nearly on her deathbed, refused it, "I know the One who created water and everything else. I will not drink such water. My trust is in my Savior Jesus Christ."

Alice was heartbroken to lose her beloved daughter in law. She began to care for her little granddaughter and kept her when John remarried.

"You know," she said to me, "A step-mother can never love another woman's child like her own. She is like my own daughter."

Alice had suffered so much sorrow and trouble. Yet through the many years I knew her, she always had a word of praise for the goodness of God, for His blessings on her and her children. Her husband, Kishin, on rare occasions said he wanted to repent of his drinking and gambling. As the preaching of the Gospel of Jesus Christ who brings hope of change continued in Jacobabad, others living there found the same joy and hope that Alice had found in Christ. For Kishin though, it was never long before he was drawn back into his old habits. By God's grace Alice continued to shine as a bright light in an otherwise very dark place. I thank God that for a short time, I was privileged to be a part of Alice's life, to know her as my sister.

7

Yasmeen
My Brahui Sister

$\mathcal{D}$ear diary," big brother Stan called out in a high falsetto voice from his sister Marilyn's room.

"No!" she screamed running toward her room at the far end of the long veranda. "Stanley! Stop! Don't you dare read my diary!"

Stan would have continued his teasing, but suddenly a tall man with a rifle came running around the corner of the house, shouting in Sindhi, "Who is hurting little Marilyn?"

Moments later I arrived on the scene to find Ali Haider standing there ready to shoot anyone–even Stanley–who might be about to hurt Marilyn! I called the two culprits out to apologize, and I explained to our faithful guard that Stan was just teasing his sister. No, there was no intruder intent on harming her.

We had recently moved into the Holland Bungalow, a large property located on the highway near the entrance to Shikarpur. The bungalow, as well as the Holland Eye Hospital a short distance away, were owned by the Anglican diocese and managed by doctors in the city of Quetta. They had been using it several weeks every winter when they brought staff from their hospital in the mountains to open the Eye Hospital. In recent years they had had to curtail their winter program. We were renting the house from them, and it was our first home in Shikarpur. Though not far out of town, there were no other homes or buildings nearby.

Since coming to Pakistan twenty years previously, we had always lived in crowded neighborhoods. We might have felt much more vulnerable on this large, more isolated property, except that it came with a large family of resident guards. This family from the Brahui tribe had moved from Quetta to guard the property. Daad, the father and head of the family, lived in a house near the gate with his two wives. His son Ali Madad was the official *chokidar*, the guard. He and his wife, Yasmeen, with their children, lived in another house behind the bungalow. His brother Ali Haider also lived there along with his family. Another brother lived just across the highway.

I had very soon gotten acquainted with the women of the family. Most of them spoke only their tribal language, but Yasmeen understood Sindhi along with a bit of Urdu. They were so hospitable that I couldn't drop in to see them without their insisting that I sit down and have a cup of tea.

One day Yasmeen asked to borrow a *charpai*, a rope bed, of which this bungalow had an abundance.

"Some guests have come and they will stay for the night," she told me. "We don't have enough beds so I thought you would let us use one."

Her round face lit up with a smile. I pointed to one on the side veranda and said, "You can take that one, but won't your husband come to carry it. It's too heavy for you."

"Oh, no!" She laughed at the idea. "I'm strong and anyway he wouldn't care. He could get another wife cheaper than buying a new water buffalo."

"What a life!" I thought as I watched her carry away the bed on her back."These women have such a hard life, and she can laugh about it." They never went outside this compound any further than across the road where their sister-in-law lived. Yet they had such a positive outlook. It was true, they really didn't know anything different. They lived almost exactly as their mothers and grandmothers had. One day I asked Yasmeen's mother-in-law how she felt about her husband taking a younger wife.

"Oh, I told him to do it," she replied. "I'm old and worn out and now she does most of the work. I just help care for her children along with the grandchildren."

When my children came home from boarding school, I took Marilyn out to introduce her to Yasmeen and the other women. Marilyn was outgoing, even as a small child, and as a teenager she loved to spend time with Pakistani women and girls. Her language skills were rudimentary, but she managed to communicate. When I took her for that first visit, Yasmeen and her sister-in-law were making flatbread for their noon meal. Each one was huge, fourteen or fifteen inches in diameter. Unlike the soft wheat *chapatis,* these were made from millet. The women baked each one on a

71

large round iron *tava* over the open fire. Several of the huge rounds were leaning against the wall next to the open fire. As we chatted, Yasmeen told me that this was the kind of bread the women usually ate. Millet was much cheaper than wheat flour. They usually made wheat chapatis for the men. I noticed that Yasmeen was preparing a small plate with curried greens for us to sample with some of the bread. I objected, saying, "No, no! We are not hungry, it's too much trouble for you!"

Yasmeen ignored me, of course, since she assumed that I was just being polite in refusing. This was the custom. One never acted eager when food was offered, so we had learned always to refuse, even several times, before finally accepting the food. Marilyn and I shared the plate, sitting on the floor of that home. We tore off pieces of bread to use as spoons, dipping it into the *saag* made from curried mustard greens. It was delicious, and Marilyn was profuse in her thanks, saying how tasty it was, how much she liked it. The bread was another story. It was so heavy we barely made a dent in the huge piece they had served us. We left to return to the house, thanking them with hugs. Yasmeen told Marilyn to come on out anytime and visit.

The next morning before my teenagers were even out of bed, I was in the kitchen with Mai, our kitchen helper. Yasmeen came to the kitchen door with a large piece of fresh millet bread and more of the curried greens.

"For Marilyn," she said. "She liked it so much."

I chuckled to myself as I went to wake her with this gift. She needed to learn not to be quite so effusive in her thanks. When it happened again the next morning, the poor girl looked at me, her eyes still sleepy, and moaned, "Oh, Mom, do I have to eat it? I do like it, but just not every morning, and I just can't eat one more bite of that bread."

Later that morning I went out to have a little chat with Yasmeen. I wasn't sure if I had been able to convince her that while we really did appreciate all the trouble they were taking to feed our daughter, she really didn't need to do this. Yasmeen didn't appear the next morning, and Marilyn learned to curb her enthusiasm when talking with Pakistanis.

After two years of living in the Holland Bungalow, we were notified by the people in Quetta that they were taking possession of the Eye Hospital from the squatters who had occupied it. They would need the bungalow again from late December through February. After we moved from this quiet refuge out on the edge of Shikarpur into the clamor and noise of the city, I continued to go back from time to time to visit Yasmeen and the other ladies. One day as I arrived at the door of the small house, I realized that other guests had arrived before me. I walked in and greeted my friends. I introduced myself to two well dressed women sitting on a charpai. They moved over and made a space for me to sit. They were local school teachers from the neighborhood primary school. I listened as they spoke in Sindhi to these illiterate women about the importance of sending their daughters to school. I didn't say much while they were there, but I was very interested to see that Yasmeen and her two sisters-in-law were nodding and smiling and agreeing that, oh, yes, girls should certainly be educated. As we drank tea together, I chatted a bit with the teachers, learning where they taught and expressing my appreciation for what they were doing in trying to get more girls enrolled in school. They got up to leave and told the Brahui ladies how much they were looking forward to seeing their girls enrolled in school in the coming term.

As soon as the teachers were out of sight, there was a burst of laughter, with all of them talking at once in Brahui, their language. Yasmeen hushed them to explain the situation to me in Sindhi, "What could we say to them? We had to agree - we are poor and ignorant and they are *begums,* upper class women. But it is impossible! Our husbands would never allow the girls to go to school. Besides, how would we ever get a husband among our people for an educated girl? It's expensive enough paying the fees and buying books and uniforms for the boys. They need to read and write and understand money. But for the girls, it will never happen!"

My heart was heavy as I returned home after that visit. These women, and the attitudes they described of their husbands, represented not just the people of their tribe, but of so many in Sindh, and other areas of Pakistan. They were intelligent, my Brahui sisters, but content, even happy the way they lived, following in the footsteps of their mothers and grandmothers.

In the late fall of 1982 as Ralph and I were sitting at the breakfast table one morning, we heard the doorbell ring. Rafiq, our gardener, came in soon after to tell us that Ali Madad and his family were outside on a donkey cart.

We both got up from the table and hurried out to the gate, wondering what was going on. Ali Madad's father had come once to show us the amazing vegetables he was growing with some American seeds we had given him. But no one else in the family had ever come.

Outside the gate we saw Yasmeen cradling her 8 year old daughter, Shahzadi, her princess. Also sitting in the cart was her mother. Ali Madad stood by the cart and began to tell us about Shahzadi's illness. She had complained of headaches and she had had a fever for some time. Now she was having a hard time walking and had been falling. This little girl who had always been so full of life and mischief, a wild thing with her hair always tangled and her clothes usually dirty and torn, lay silent in her mother's arms. She recognized me and tried to smile.

Ali Madad wanted a note from us to the doctor at the Christian Hospital, thinking that would get them better treatment. Ralph went inside to write the note while I explained that they didn't need a note. Coming in a donkey cart was a bit like arriving at an American hospital's Emergency Department in an ambulance. Coming in such a conveyance signalled that someone was seriously ill, a person who couldn't stand in line, a patient the doctors would see immediately. They left with the note and our assurance that we both would come over to the hospital as soon as we could.

On hearing the symptoms and checking the little girl over, Dr. Maybel concluded that she likely had TB meningitis and started her on treatment. The small hospital was not equipped to do sophisticated testing.

Marilyn had come back to Shikarpur in the fall to work for a short term at the hospital. Her planned year came to an end after only three months when she was unable to get an extension on her visa. She and I rode a tonga to the Holland Bungalow before Christmas to visit with Yasmeen. I hoped to see Shahazadi healthy again and running around, but found that she was still not well.

I returned again after a few weeks to find that she was much worse. The medications were not helping at all. I persuaded the family that they needed to take her back to the hospital and promised to return in the afternoon in our car to drive them over. I talked with the doctor before going back to get them. They would admit her to the hospital to keep an eye on her and see what they could do. Her grandmother stayed with the little girl, sleeping in the bed with her. The child had probably never slept a night alone in her whole life. I was working in the hospital at the time directing the spiritual ministries so I stopped by the ward regularly for the next few days. Her granny took such loving care of that little girl and the family sent food over every day. Shahzadi was cleaner than I had ever seen her. But I could see that she was a very sick child.

Dr. Jocelyn took me aside one day and said, "I'm quite sure she has a brain tumor. We thought of sending them to Karachi, but they don't know anyone there. And even if they could go, I doubt if they could get any real help. Even with western medicine, there isn't much we can do for childhood brain tumors. We need to send them home because Shahzadi is going to die, and they won't want her to die away from home."

She asked if Ralph would come over in the afternoon and bring Ali Madad, Shahzadi's father, so she could speak with him. She wanted us there when she gave him the bad news. Later that day we stood next to the hospital bed as Dr. Jocelyn gently told Ali Madad and his mother-in-law that the little girl had a growth in her brain and she would not live many more days. There was nothing she or the other doctor could do.

Ali Madad's mother cried silent tears. There was no wailing as she held her granddaughter and stroked her head. Shahzadi's father, this strong, hardened man who ostensibly didn't care much for girls anyway, stood, stoic in his grief. But then I saw something I had never seen in Pakistan, a Muslim man shedding tears for his daughter his little princess.

A couple of weeks later, we received a message that Shahzadi had died. We went over that evening, with Dr. Ann and Hannah, one of the nurses from the hospital. After seeming to rally and improve somewhat, the girl had lapsed into a coma and died before dawn that day. They had buried her immediately as is the custom. We expressed our sympathy, and I shed tears as I hugged each of the women. I held Yasmeen a bit longer. While we sat with them, they allowed Ralph to read from John 14 and to pray for them in the name of Jesus.

Then Daad, Shahzadi's grandfather stood up, raised his hands in prayer, "Oh Allah, have mercy on us! We kill and steal and cheat. We are on the wrong path! Show us the right path."

Ralph and I continued to pray for these people we loved, "How long, Oh Lord? Open the eyes of these dear people to see Jesus as the right path, the Way to know the Father."

*M*y daughter Marilyn returned to Pakistan for flood relief work as a nurse in the fall of 2010. During her two weeks in Shikarpur she met many of the women who had known me during our years of living there. She told me later that she was determined to get back to the Holland

Bungalow to see Yasmeen before she left. I had not realized how deeply Marilyn had been affected by her own friendship with this Brahui woman. Not much older than my teenage daughter, Yasmeen already had three children at that time. Marilyn went by *tonga*, a horse and buggy taxi, from the hospital compound through the city, past the Holland Eye Hospital and across the railway tracks. She rode out to the highway on the edge of the city, and arrived at the gate of the Holland Bungalow property. She walked the long driveway to the bungalow, unoccupied and looking dusty and neglected. Then she rounded the corner to the small house out back.

Marilyn writes, "As we approached her home at the back of the large compound, Yasmeen came running out, tears in her eyes. She began blessing me, over and over she uttered the words, *"Allah muhabat, Allah jo Shukr ahay, Bismillah."* She hugged and blessed, her hand on my head. It was a greeting of biblical proportions." [1]

During that visit, Yasmeen brought out a small photo album with pictures of our family that I had given her, now faded. In the short two years we had lived in that house as neighbors, we had become friends and our love had blossomed. My sister, Yasmeen, unbeknownst to me, had become my daughter's sister. Oh that the eyes of her heart, the hearts of each one in this whole extended family, this tribe of Brahui people, might be opened to see the love of God in Jesus Christ for them!

---

1   Marilyn Gardner, Worlds Apart (Cambridge, MA Doorlight Publications, 2018), 181

8

Fareeda
Would-Be Feminist

We were expecting a new doctor, a woman in her fifties. Ann would spend her first year studying Sindhi full time. As the supervisor of Sindhi language students, I had the responsibility of finding individual tutors. Educated young women, living at home waiting for their parents to arrange a marriage, were often happy for this opportunity. Teaching a young foreign woman added a bit of excitement to their lives. Their willingness to become friends was a great advantage to the new missionary in learning the culture and giving opportunities to speak and hear Sindhi outside of formal classes.

But for Ann a young woman really wouldn't do. A younger woman would be reluctant to correct an older woman, and Ann was a doctor, inviting an extra layer of respect. I remembered that Ameena, my seamstress, had an unmarried sister approaching middle age. They lived in our neighborhood, so I sent word that I would like to have Fareeda come to see me.

When she came, we sat in my living room drinking tea and chatting about our families, about Fareeda's work as a primary school teacher and, as always, about the weather. Then I asked if she would consider teaching Sindhi to our new doctor who would be arriving soon. I told her that Dr. Ann Irish would be living with us for the next several months.

Her answer surprised me, coming from a woman who went out to work every day. "I have to get my brother's permission," she said. "My father is gone and my brother is head of the house. He will ask me if there will be any young men in the house when I am here."

I assured her, "My sons are all in America. Only my husband is living here with me and we have Rafiq, our gardener and *chokidar*, but he works outside. You will be safe and we will respect your customs."

Fareeda sent me a message a few days later that her brother had given permission. I shook my head, wondering to myself if I would ever really understand this conservative culture. Fareeda was a middle-aged woman, working and supporting the family, probably at least as much as her brother did. He was several years younger, yet she had to ask permission to take a part time job tutoring a middle-aged woman in our home.

After Ann arrived and had settled into our guestroom, I invited Fareeda to meet her. As we sat drinking tea in the living room, the two women seemed to bond immediately. Their personalities were similar, both rather blunt and outspoken. There would be no problem of this teacher being reluctant to correct her student. After we finished tea, and before Fareeda left, we set up a schedule for her to come four afternoons a week. As she got up to leave, I invited her to see Ann's room and the small sitting area just outside it. We had hung a curtain in the open doorway to the living room as well as another curtain to block the hall to Ralph's office. He could enter or leave his office through our bedroom which had a door to the veranda. With his gray hair, Ralph was not one of the "young men" she, and her brother, were concerned about, but I was able to assure her that she would be safe from any male eyes as she sat with Ann for their lessons.

Ann had arrived in October and seemed to be progressing nicely. The Sindhi language is difficult, both in pronunciation and grammar, and it was slow-going. But the two women had become fast friends, and Fareeda had invited Ann to her home several times. She had become "Our Dr. Ann" to the whole family, including Fareeda's nieces and nephews. Ann developed great rapport with the children.

*C*hristmas was coming, with its teas and celebrations. Our house was surrounded by a large compound and at the far end there were small houses where Rafiq, with his family, and several hospital employees lived. Most of these families were from the Marwari tribe and they all spoke Sindhi as well as their own language. There was no shortage of children, and Ralph and I planned a party for them during the week following Christmas. When Ann suggested inviting Fareeda's nephews and nieces to the party, I hesitated. Muslims in Pakistan generally don't mix socially with those they consider "low caste." The Marwari families, coming from a poor

Hindu background, were definitely in that category. I tried to explain to Ann the complicated social structures we had sought to navigate through our years of experience.

Ann and I decided that she would invite her teacher to bring her nieces and nephews to the party, explaining about the other children we were inviting. There would also be some other Muslim children coming from the family of Sadorah my kitchen helper. Fareeda could take the invitation home and let the family decide whether they wanted to let the children come or not.

I was pleasantly surprised when Fareeda came back to say that the children were very excited to come to "Our Dr. Ann's party!" The day came and we had a yard full of children. Ralph and I had planned races and games for them with small prizes. As he gave instructions in Sindhi to the children, dividing them into teams, Fareeda was there wearing her brown silk *burka,* covered from head to foot. She had thrown back her face veil, and she repeated everything Ralph said to the children, apparently thinking they might not understand his Sindhi. Fareeda was nearly as excited as the children. When we finished all the planned races and games, I was ready to invite the children into the veranda for tea and sweets.

"Wait," Fareeda called out. "Dr. Ann and I want to race, let us race." She threw off her burka, and tied her *dupatta,* her headscarf, around her neck so it wouldn't fall off. She lined herself up with Dr. Ann and nodded to Ralph to give them the signal. Off they ran to the end of the yard and turned to run back. It was a tie between the Doctor and her teacher, and I don't know which of them was more delighted with this children's party.

When we were helping Ann make plans to spend four months out of the heat of Sindh in the cool of the Murree Hills in the north of Pakistan, she proposed that she take Fareeda with her for the two months of her vacation from teaching. As I hesitated, Ann insisted that she had thought this plan out quite thoroughly.

"She can live with me, we'll cook and eat together and I really want to do this. I think I'll learn more Sindhi this way."

No one had ever done this before. The other tutors were all Sindhi men. All the Sindhi students would be organized into a small language school. Would Ann really be better off with her teacher living with her? I was her language supervisor so the decision was really in my hands. However, Ann was not a young single missionary. She was in her fifties and knew what she wanted. So Fareeda spent two months with Ann in Murree, and their friendship deepened. It was quite an experience for Fareeda since she had not been further from home than the city of Hyderabad in southern Sindh. To see the mountains, the pine trees and the green landscape, to walk the hill roads and paths of Murree, this was all so new to her. It hardly ever rains in Sindh, and Fareeda experienced the monsoon rains for the first time.

When Ann returned to Sindh in September, she moved into her own apartment at the hospital and began to work part-time. She continued to study with Fareeda several afternoons a week. As they began to read from the New Testament in Sindhi, Fareeda was exposed to the Gospel and our Christian beliefs about Jesus as the Son of God, His atoning death on the cross, and His rising from the dead. For the first time she was reading the New Testament. And she shared with Ann the Muslim denial of these core truths of the Gospel. Fareeda, like so many Muslims, appreciated her friendship with Ann, with me, and with other missionaries. The women in the family took advantage of the medical care they could receive from the Christian Hospital for themselves and for their children.

When Ann realized the need for health education for women coming to the hospital, she arranged for several health booklets to be translated from Urdu to Sindhi. At her invitation Fareeda checked the Sindhi translation with her. One was a booklet with information and advice for pregnant women. A short paragraph near the beginning explained how the sex of the child is determined.

After reading this, Fareeda stopped, looked up at Ann, and asked, "Is this really true? Does the man's seed really decide if the baby is a boy or a girl?"

Ann replied, "Of course it's true. We don't publish anything that isn't true."

Fareeda was livid. "Do you know how many women are blamed because they have a girl when their husband wants a son? Everyone thinks it's the woman's fault. We should do something about this. We should print it on posters and put them in every railway station and all the bazaars in Sindh!"

As they talked about it, both women recognized the impossibility of ever doing such a thing in Sindh.

"But we never know," Ann continued, "When a woman takes this book home, her husband may read it and learn from it.

Ann asked Fareeda's advice about whether it would be proper for her, a woman, to read through the booklets with the Muslim Sindhi translator who worked with Ralph on the New Testament.

"Why not?" Fareeda laughed. "You and I aren't supposed to know about any of this because we have never been married. Perhaps from reading this he will learn something and tell some other men."

Even though Fareeda could accept these medical facts, her heart and mind remained closed to the Christian Gospel. She was a dear sister in so many ways, but I longed to see the Holy Spirit at work to open the eyes of her heart.

*D*uring our last months in Pakistan, I made a special effort to visit many of my friends, knowing that my time was limited. Then I fell, injuring my back, The Doctor put me on three weeks bed rest. As I lay flat on my back, I wondered how I would see all those women I wanted to visit. During those three weeks, many of them heard of my injury and came to see me. Fareeda was one of them.

I had not often seen her alone, but here in my bedroom, as we drank the tea that Sadorah, my helper, brought to us, I had perhaps the deepest conversation I had ever had with her. We talked of her faith, and she listened as I shared my trust in God through my faith in Isa Masih, Jesus.

Just before we left Pakistan, Fareeda came again to see me, bringing a gift. It was a small, very lovely, handmade rug. She unrolled it, and I noticed that it had a direction in the pattern, and was just the size Muslims use for praying as they face Mecca. She wanted me to know that this was not a prayer rug, and insisted that I understand this. I didn't understand, but I simply thanked her, admiring the handcrafted piece. I value this gift, and I have tucked that puzzling conversation away in my heart along with the many other gaps in my comprehension of my Muslim sisters' thinking. Often when I step onto this small rug beside my bed, I thank God for the relationship He enabled us to have with this sister, and I continue to pray for His work in Fareeda's life.

9

Sakina
Hidden Jewel

My heart sank, but I hid my disappointment. Ralph and I had been impressed with Sakhavat, the new pastor called by the Larkana church. He had been working as an evangelist in a medical program near the Indian border. Because of tensions between India and Pakistan, that program had been curtailed indefinitely. Sakhavat moved his family into the city of Hyderabad temporarily. After meeting Sakhavat and hearing him preach, the people of St. Stephen's Church in Larkana believed that God had called him to be our new pastor.

I first met his wife Sakina when he moved his family to Larkana, and Ralph brought the family into our living room for a cup of tea. I had such a clear idea of what this Pastor's wife should be, and Sakina did not fit the picture. I wanted an educated woman who could relate to the Christian nurses working at the Civil Hospital as well as the other women in our congregation. With her poor eyesight, her thick glasses and her bent and crippled body, Sakina was anything but impressive. I soon learned that she was illiterate. God and I apparently had very different ideas of what the church needed in a pastor's wife.

Before long though, I learned her story, and behind the unassuming appearance, I discovered a precious jewel, a sister in Christ with a vibrant faith. Early in their marriage, Sakina had developed rheumatoid arthritis. One of her legs had become locked in a bent position, leaving her unable to walk, except for hobbling around her home with a stick. Sakhavat actually carried her on his back to church every Sunday. He continued to do this in spite of the ridicule they suffered each week. Even some Christian friends told him he should divorce her and get a useful wife. Eventually they heard that the doctors at the Women's Hospital in the city of Multan might be able to help Sakina. Sakhavat took his wife by train to Multan to the hospital where she was treated with love and compassion. She stayed for some time at the hospital after having surgery to straighten her leg and to get regulated on medication for the pain she suffered. The leg would be permanently stiff, but now she could walk although with a decided limp.

While at the hospital Sakina fell in love with a toddler, an orphan named Ruthie, born there and abandoned by her mother. Ruthie's thyroid gland did not function and she required daily replacement medication. She had become the pet of the hospital staff as well as the patients. Sakina's heart went out to this motherless child, and she asked about adopting her. In the end she insisted that she would not go home unless Ruthie went with her. Her husband, Sakhavat, had to consent. The hospital administrators decided that they were not likely to find a more loving family for their beloved Ruthie and gave her for adoption by her new parents.

When the family moved to Larkana, Ruthie was ten with two younger siblings, a sister Parveen and a brother Sammy. All the children went to school and Ruthie had become her mother's capable helper. She could cook and clean and had boundless energy. She was such a happy child, always with a big smile. With her thyroid problem, Ruthie would have died if she had been born at home in a village. But God in His mercy had spared her and brought her into Sakina's life to bless the whole family.

Every Sunday morning after the church service, the courtyard of their home was buzzing with activity. A number of off-duty nurses, and other women from the congregation often dropped in. Sakina sat on a *charpai,* a rope strung bed covered with a colorful Sindhi *ajrak,* the traditional hand-blocked cloth. She seemed in her element. As Ruthie, with her little sister Parveen's help, served tea and cookies to each guest, Sakina listened and joined in the conversation, often in the Punjabi language. As she listened, Sakina served up loving advice, often along with a scripture verse from memory. Sometimes she would place her arm around one of the nurses and pray for her concerns. The younger women called her Auntie, and to the older women she was Sister.

I often found my way across the yard that separated our homes to sit with Sakina, to read the Bible, and to pray together. On hot days in the late afternoon I sometimes looked out to see her walking around the paths enjoying the flowers, the grass, and the shade of the large Neem tree. The Lord had shown me once again how wrong it is to judge by appearances. Sakina's crippled body housed a beautiful soul, and God used her in remarkable ways to bless so many, including me.

One day boys coming out of the mosque behind their home began tossing rocks over the wall into Sakhavat and Sakina's courtyard. Someone on the street chased the boys away, and no damage was done, but the incident was disturbing. After I heard about it, I went over to talk with Sakina. With all her physical problems, with the pain she lived with, she praised God that He had protected the children. The stones had fallen harmlessly on the floor of the courtyard.

"Oh, yes," she told me, "our Lord is so good! He protected us from those who would hurt us, and He will continue to do it."

We all gathered right there where the stones had fallen to praise God for His protection.

Those four years in Larkana were good years for Sakina and her family. Initially I had struggled with moving from the large city of Hyderabad back to Upper Sindh. Earlier in our life in Pakistan, I had said, "I never want to live in Larkana, but if I have to, please, not the Baker Building." But God had sent us there and yes, we were living in the Baker Building, right in the center of the city, across from the Cinema with it's noisy crowds late into the night. God had joy for us right there in the place where I never wanted to live, and one of the greatest was my friendship with my sister Sakina.

After four years we went to the US for an extended home assignment. On our return to Pakistan we would have been happy to return to Larkana, but we were asked to move to Shikarpur. The church in Larkana seemed healthy under Sakhavat's ministry. We planned regular visits to keep in touch until Connie and Larry Johnson moved there in 1981. Sakhavat was a deeply spiritual man but he also took life very seriously. He became progressively more depressed and paranoid. Previously he had boldly talked with Muslims about Jesus and the Gospel, and some had called him to come to their homes to pray for healing. But now he became more and more fearful. In the 1980s he was hospitalized in Lahore, and Sakina and the children moved back to southern Punjab where relatives took them in. Sakina only lived a few more years before God took her.

An uncle arranged Ruthie's marriage to a widower with three children. Ralph and I attended the wedding and saw a radiantly happy bride. Brides in Pakistan are not supposed to look happy, but Ruthie's irrepressible joy in life and in the Lord could not be hidden. When I hugged her, she said, "Auntie, God is giving me a family, children to love. He is so good to me." With her long term physical problems she had been told that she would not be able to have children. But God had other plans and a couple of years later we heard that she was pregnant and delivered a healthy baby boy. Sakina's love and compassion for this orphaned little girl was bearing much fruit.

I continue to thank God for the lessons He taught me through my sister Sakina, for the beauty I found beneath an unassuming exterior, for the many ways He used such a humble vessel, His jewel, Sakina, for His glory.

10

Meena
Light in a Dark Place

Meena grew up in a Hindu family in the mixed Hindu and Christian colony of sweepers in Shikarpur. A bright, pretty girl, she started working as a cleaner at Shikarpur Christian Hospital when she was in her teens. I first encountered her there, her petite form bent over a broom in one of the wards. Like most women, she wore her shiny black hair pulled back into a bun at the back of her head. She stood up and, seeing me, her round face broke into a smile, her dark eyes sparkling. We chatted briefly. I learned her name and that she had recently begun working at the hospital.

Meena was not shy. She loved working in the hospital where there were always patients to chat with as she worked. While many of the Pakistani nurses and aides were reticent with foreigners, Meena was outgoing and considered everyone her friend. When my daughter Marilyn came to work as a short term nurse, the two became fast friends.

Meena knew no English, and Marilyn's Urdu was basic, but the two, both outgoing, had no problem communicating during the few months Marilyn was there.

Carol and Joanna, nurses who came to the hospital in 1983, also became friends of Meena. They visited her home and invited her to theirs for tea. Meena, with her outgoing personality, shared her story with her new friends. She had never gone to school. Some of the Christian girls in the colony where she lived had learned to read through adult literacy classes. After earning their certificates, those girls had entered a class at the hospital and were now working as Nurse Aides. Perhaps she had been too young, or perhaps her Hindu parents discouraged it, but she had not learned to read at that time. The classes had been discontinued and she was working full time as a cleaner.

Meena had become a Christian and wanted to be able to read the Bible. Joanna ordered adult literacy books and began tutoring her after work. Most days the two sat together over a literacy book at the kitchen table in Joanna's apartment. Meena was bright and learned quickly.

At that time an older couple, Bob and Justina Wiebe, came to the hospital. While Bob worked on plumbing problems, Justina helped out in various ways. In spite of their knowing no Urdu, they became friends with Meena. When she invited them to come for tea, she asked Ralph and me to come along with them.

Meena asked Ralph to pray before we left, and she called her whole family in. As we were leaving, she whispered to me, "I pray every night that everyone in my family will become Christian."

Meena had reached the age when her parents wanted to arrange her marriage. She had already refused one arrangement they had tried to make.

"I'm a Christian," she said firmly. "I can't marry a Hindu."

She had wanted to be baptized the previous Easter, but her parents were really upset by this and refused their permission. Her job at the Christian hospital was a good thing in their opinion. It was a safe place for a young woman to work and if she went to church, there was no harm in that. But through her association with the Christians at the hospital, Meena's life had been changed. She now had a relationship with God through her faith in Christ. Baptism, however, was a legal step in Pakistan. She would no longer be a Hindu but a Christian. This they could not allow. Her father was so disturbed that he went to talk with his brother. After years of not speaking, they made up their longstanding enmity because of Meena's stubbornness, and vowed that no one in their family would ever become a Christian.

Meena was feeling the pressure, realizing that she couldn't keep on refusing to marry. Her father began talking with a Hindu acquaintance who had a son of the right age. This family lived in the city of Quetta. In God's providence this young man had become a Roman Catholic Christian.

As the two men talked, Meena's father said, "My daughter is this way…"

The friend replied, "Well, it so happens that my son is also…"

Over the next few weeks, as the arrangements were being made, Meena realized that she could not expect any better arrangement so she consented to the engagement. Seema, her younger sister was also being married at the same time, and the date for the double wedding was set.

Meena left her work at the hospital several weeks before she was to be married. During the last week before the wedding, she was confined to a room in her home, not allowed to go out. The ceremony was on a Thursday evening, and I went with a group from the hospital. Carol, Joanna and I, along with Hannah, a senior nurse, and Barb Gustafson, a young Canadian, went in to see Meena, still confined to the house. When the others went out to dinner, I stayed behind for a few minutes alone with Meena. She told me that during the days when she had to stay inside, she had been reading the New Testament that Joanna had given her.

"The Lord showed me some very precious verses," she said, and continued, "People are telling me that I won't be a Christian anymore because of all these Hindu ceremonies. But God knows my heart. These are just the customs of men. I have to do it because of my parents. I don't want to, and I've been praying that somehow I can be a good witness."

I was amazed at the strength of Meena's faith, and the spiritual insights and discernment she demonstrated as such a young believer.

Most of the hospital staff were invited to the wedding. Unlike other weddings we had attended, the meal was served before the ceremony, and many people left after eating. Carol, Joanna and I stayed, along with Hannah and Barb. We were sitting in the room with Meena and her sister when the women came in to dress them. Seema began to cry and scream. At first Meena cried quietly, but soon both girls were crying and screaming. Joanna and Carol were sitting on either side of Meena. She cried over and over, "Bhaji Carol, Bhaji Joanna, help me."

Pakistani brides are expected to act sad because they are leaving their parents and the only home they have ever known. But I had never seen anything like this scene. By the time two uncles came in to take them out, it sounded as if someone had died! Meena had such a tender conscience that I wondered if part of her problem was realizing that she had to take part in the Hindu ceremony. Each uncle lifted up one of the girls and tossed her over his shoulder, "Just like a couple of sacks of rice," I thought.

Outside there was an enclosure with four sticks at the corners with string around three sides. In the enclosure a clay lamp was lit with four wicks burning. Each of the couples walked around this lamp seven times. Four times the groom led his bride and three times the bride led the groom. Meena had to be helped by some of the relatives, and they were practically carrying her, passing her from one to the other. The Hindu priest offered prayers, and at the end of the ceremonies, her uncle carried Meena back into the house. When we saw her before we left, she had calmed down and seemed quite happy.

This whole experience opened my eyes to the power and influence that Hinduism still has in a mixed colony like this one. Perhaps half the people living there profess to be Christians. Among them are some who understand their faith and are really trying to live as Christians. They are truly lights in a very dark place. But they daily face temptations and pressures from the hostile environment. Meena would be living in a very similar situation in her new home in Quetta.

Before Meena left Shikarpur, she and Daud, her new husband, came to our home for tea. She showed no sadness, but was again the happy, fun-loving Meena we had known. When I embraced her, she whispered to me, "It's good, Auntie. God has given me a good husband."

Some months later, Carol and Joanna came to me. They reminded me that they had promised Meena they would visit her in Quetta. Would I be willing to go with them? They arranged time off from the hospital and we set a time with Meena through an exchange of letters. She had not progressed to writing, but Daud could read and write, so he wrote on Meena's behalf. The date was set and we made our train reservations. We traveled on the Quetta Passenger, a night train. What a night it was! Our compartment had four berths, and the fourth passenger was an overly friendly, retired army officer. We had settled in our berths, the lights were off, and I was dozing when the cover to the ceiling fan crashed to the floor. Our fellow passenger leaped up in the dark shouting, "What is it? Oh, my God Almighty!"

We didn't get much sleep, but our train arrived on time at the Quetta Railway Station. On the platform we met Daud who had come to meet us on his bicycle. We would have been more comfortable staying with friends and just visiting Meena and Daud. But Carol and Joanna were eager to stay with Meena in her home. We were soon riding on a tonga to the sweeper colony where Meena waited for us. Their small house had only one room and a small courtyard. Entering their bedroom/sitting room we immediately saw pictures of Hindu gods on the walls on all sides, dominating the room. I was disappointed, but not surprised. We chatted with Daud about his family and how he had become a Christian. For the few days of this visit, we were privileged to enter Meena's world, to see and experience life as she lived it.

Fifty or more homes lined the sides around a large open space, and we soon learned that there was one communal latrine for all these people. Meena was embarrassed that she had nothing better to offer us. When we went to the latrine, a crowd of children and women followed us, waiting outside until we came out. Although we had no privacy for going to the latrine, Meena insisted we eat alone in the room while she sat outside in the courtyard. We strongly objected, refusing to eat unless she came in and ate with us.

There is so much life in a colony like this, with laughing or crying children, bleating goats, and neighbors calling out to one another. We saw amazingly little fighting among the children.

But where are the signs of spiritual life? As a child of God, Meena seemed alone. Daud professed to be a believer, but did he have the desire to grow, and to help Meena to grow? Would the Lord use her with her lovely personality and her strong faith to be a light in this place? Could that faith survive?

During the three days we were with her, we took Meena to visit two of the Christian nurse aides who had moved from Shikarpur to Quetta after their marriages. Both were living in another sweeper colony across the city. Naseem's husband was a Roman Catholic believer; Nasreen was married to a Hindu. How could these two young women, how could anyone, live a real Christian life in such an environment, where pictures of Hindu gods hung on the walls of their homes, loud disco music blared long into the night, and gambling and alcohol abuse were pervasive.

We visited Meena in April, when Quetta was still cold during the night and in the early morning. I woke early and huddled by Meena's fire in the corner of the courtyard, drinking chai out of a little glass. We talked about her life, and about Nasreen, who had begged her parents not to make her marry a Hindu. Carol and Joanna awoke, and Carol bravely bathed with cold water in a corner of the courtyard that Meena had curtained off for us. Joanna and I opted to just have a wash. The waste water ran out into an open drain.

On Sunday we tried to find a church, and found Daud unhelpful. We finally found a Pentecostal church, but the service was nearly over when we arrived. There we met an American couple, who were shocked that we were staying in the sweeper colony rather than with foreigners. I smiled and replied that Meena was a Christian and a friend, and we wanted to encourage her.

Meena was making *chapatis* for our lunch when we returned. Later in the afternoon, we all went to Daud's sister's home. Married to a Roman Catholic, she had no Hindu pictures on her walls, and she told us, "My children are growing up as Christians."

Each evening before going to bed, we read from the Bible and prayed with Meena. Daud sat out in the courtyard where he could hear it all. Perhaps because we were all women he was uncomfortable joining us. But on our last evening Daud played the flute for us, demonstrating considerable talent. We said goodbye to Meena the following day to return to our own lives, thankful for the opportunity to enter in for this brief time into Meena's world.

During our visit with Meena, we had seen two partridges shut up in a tiny courtyard. They strutted round and round in a small circle, craning their necks up to the square of blue sky far above the courtyard walls. But their wings were clipped, they were prisoners within the four walls. Like Meena.

She was so bright, and so desired to live a Christian life. She knows God through her faith in His Son Jesus. Yet her world was so small, so confined. How could she grow, living this way? I take heart, because I know that God's Spirit is not bound. I prayed that, whatever her outward circumstances, Meena would know the true freedom in Christ that God has promised to His children.

11

Sheila
Lover of God

When I was a child in Winchendon, Massachusetts, I first heard about India from a missionary who came to our small Baptist Church. Around that same time, Sheila was born into a Christian family in South India. Her maternal grandparents had been among the first converts from Hinduism in that area. As often happens with the second generation, her parents were part of the Christian community, but they had only a superficial faith without a personal relationship with God.

Sheila's father traveled a great deal in his job. Her mother, along with their children, lived with her parents in a two room house in the city of Bangalore. As a small child Sheila slept on a mat with her grandmother. Waking up each morning she saw her grandma already up, sitting with hands folded in front of a picture of Jesus, praying and kissing the picture. Her earliest memories of Jesus date to those early mornings of her childhood.

As the eldest child Sheila was her Grandma's shadow as she went through her day. The house had no electricity or running water, and she helped with chores, like carrying water from the public tap and starting the wood fire in the tiny, ramshackle kitchen where her grandmother cooked meals for the whole family. At dusk, her grandfather, sitting on a mat in the front room began singing "Abide with Me, fast falls the eventide," and the family gathered around him for prayers.

"All of us sat on the floor," Sheila recalls, "singing those grand old hymns of the church, some in English, others in Tamil, the language of the area. Grandpa read from the Bible and prayed. We ended praying the Lord's Prayer together and reciting from Psalm 103:1-5. On Sundays we all went to the nearby Lutheran Church and thus I passed the first nine years of my life."

In 1947, Britain granted independence to India, and the country was partitioned into two. A new country, Pakistan, was created as a homeland for the Muslims of the Indian subcontinent. Sheila's father had begun working in a bank in the northwest of India, which became Pakistan. Following partition her mother moved the family to join her father there.

Sheila often felt overwhelmed. As the eldest she had a lot of responsibilities, but she carried on, coping with this new country and a new language, Urdu. Studying in a Catholic Convent School gave her a good foundation in English. The British nuns who taught in the school instilled in her a love of the language and of learning. She loved to read and study. At home her family often spoke English, but also continued to speak Tamil as well. In Karachi they attended English services at the Methodist Church. But for Sheila her faith never really spilled over into her personal life. If she prayed, it was mostly just token prayers.

Four more siblings were born after the move to Pakistan. Two of her brothers died young, and Sheila saw her Mum bearing the sorrow pretty much alone. How she must have missed being surrounded by her extended family so far away in South India.

Her father's job involved frequent transfers to new cities, leaving Sheila feeling rootless, with no real friends, as if she was just drifting. In 1962, her parents took her back to India to arrange her marriage to Winston, who would be her husband for the next 55 years. This was an enormous change for Sheila. Her parents returned to Pakistan, leaving her to make a new life with Winston and his family. However difficult life seemed to Sheila during that time, God had begun to work out His purposes for her.

She remembers, "It was through my husband's family that I began my journey of a personal relationship with Jesus Christ as my Lord and Savior. I saw Winston's family living out their faith in their daily life and this was all new to me. The fact that Jesus Christ gave His life for me, I remember weeping that someone loved me so much that He died for me so I could be His child and be free! I was really excited about the reality of my new relationship with God."

Sheila's sister-in-law became her spiritual guide, teaching her to pray and to trust God, to daily confess and repent of sin. She felt excited with this new relationship with God, but she was still unhappy living in India, homesick for her own family far away in Pakistan. According to custom, Sheila returned to her parents' home for the birth of their first child, John. After his birth she made the decision to stay in Pakistan, and Winston left his family in India to be with his wife and son.

Sheila was soon wondering if she had made a big mistake. There were tensions with her family over integrity issues. Sheila and Winston stood firm, determined to live out their faith in their work as well as at home. They found this more difficult in Muslim Pakistan than in South India where Christians were more numerous. Eventually though, her family all became believers, and a sense of family and love was restored. Winston and Sheila had two more children, Joanna and James, born in Karachi.

During these years Sheila was introduced to the Pakistan Bible Correspondence School. She began to study our English courses. Ralph was principal of the school, and he recruited me to correct the courses for the few women students enrolled. I first met Sheila through correcting her lessons, and I was struck by the sincerity that came through her answers. She often had questions. I wrote my answers and comments on her lessons, and I often enclosed a personal note when mailing it back. Sheila was growing so much in her understanding of the Bible as she continued to study the lessons.

In 1972 a neighbor told Sheila about Central Baptist Church, and they began attending the English services as a family. Sheila learned that a women's Bible Study was being held in a home right in her neighborhood. As she began to attend, she became acquainted with the teacher, Grace Pittman. She also met other Christian women, including Ruth Montgomery. These women encouraged Sheila in her faith, and she was able to ask questions and discuss with them what she was learning in her Correspondence School studies. On our occasional trips to Karachi, Ralph and I stayed with the Montgomerys or the Pittmans, so before long I was able to meet this woman who had become my favorite student. I learned much later how excited Sheila was to meet me, the teacher who had corrected her lessons and corresponded with her, sending encouraging notes. I was also thrilled to finally meet the woman I had only known through correspondence.

Our friendship grew and several times we stayed in Sheila and Winston's home when we visited Karachi. Occasionally they hosted our whole family, a challenge for them in their small apartment. Our children have wonderful memories of Sheila's delicious meals, and they sometimes still use her recipes when they cook Pakistani meals.

Sheila shared her concern for their children's education. She knew that our children were studying at Murree Christian School. Her friend Ruth Montgomery also had children who had studied there. Ruth's children were older, but our younger two were still in school. They decided to send their children, John, Joanna and later James, to Murree Christian School. John was in my son Dan's class. My daughter Marilyn and her husband were boarding parents for their son Jim for a year.

Through all of our shared life and experiences, Sheila has become a life long friend, a precious sister in Christ. Through Winston's experience as an accountant, he was able to get a job in Dubai and they moved from Karachi. Their children all went to college in the US, and eventually Sheila and Winston emigrated to Canada. What a surprise several years later to hear from my daughter that she had met Jim and his wife at their church in Phoenix. The next time Ralph and I visited Marilyn and Cliff, we learned that Sheila and Winston were also visiting Phoenix. What a joy to reconnect after so many years, to share chai and a meal together, and to talk about the ways God has blessed both of us with his loving care through all these years of our friendship. Since then I have been able to stay in touch with Sheila through technology, learning of Winston's death only weeks before my husband passed away. I have prayed and agonized with her through her daughter Joanna's cancer treatment, to rejoice with her when I heard that Joanna is in remission. Yes, Sheila has been, and still is my precious sister in Christ, a true "lover of God."

12

Elishba and Mukhtar:
Bright Gems

Elishba and Mukhtar had finished high school, and they wanted to enroll in a Bible Institute in a nearby city. But would their parents permit it?

The two were cousins who had grown up like sisters in a Punjabi Christian community in Lahore, the largest city in Punjab Province. While growing up they had both come to faith in Christ. They had recently learned that a man named Lal Din had started a Bible Institute in a city not far from Lahore and was accepting women into his school. Not many girls in their Christian community attended school as long as Elishba and Mukhtar had. Their parents were likely thinking of possible marriage arrangements for them. Elishba and Mukhtar were determined, and with their parents' permission both girls enrolled in the three year course.

Our co-workers Larry and Connie Johnson had moved to the Bible Institute to teach. While Larry taught,

Connie, a nurse, cared for the minor physical needs of the students. She mothered all of them, but especially the few single women at the school. One of the Johnsons' hopes in spending time away from our work in Sindh was to inspire some Punjabi Christians with a vision for the great spiritual needs of Sindhi Muslims. Mukhtar immediately caught this vision, convinced that the Lord was calling her to work with Sindhi women. She and Elishba began to pray for Sindh and especially for the women.

Following graduation Elishba and Mukhtar worked in Lahore with Child Evangelism Fellowship and in Adult Literacy Programs. Their burden for the needs of Sindhi women only grew stronger, but they did not see how two young single women could move so far away. Their families would not allow it.

After the Johnsons returned to Shikarpur, Connie became convinced it was time to do something about the illiteracy among the women and girls in the local sweeper colony. Many of the teenage girls had never gone to school or had dropped out after two or three years and remained illiterate. She remembered Elishba and Mukhtar as two shining lights in their bible School class. On receiving Connie's invitation, the two young women persuaded their parents to let them go to work in Shikarpur. They knew God had called them to Sindh.

In Shikarpur Elishba and Mukhtar lived in the nurses' hostel behind the hospital. Each day in the early afternoon the two young women gathered their books and equipment to go by tonga to hold a class in the sweeper colony. There was a good response and a number of the girls learned to read and earned their certificates.

Often in the mornings the two could be found in the hospital talking and praying with women patients or their relatives. Soon they were learning Sindhi and within a couple of years they were working full-time in the hospital, leading the daily worship and visiting the women patients. Their families objected strongly when they realized that their daughters were actually visiting in Muslim homes. But God's call was so strong that Mukhtar, one day in relating this to another missionary, cried and said, "How can we not go to them? They need to know about God's love in Jesus."

When the hospital established the position of Director of Spiritual Ministries, I was asked to take it. My responsibilities included oversight of the Chapel programs, the bookstore, manned by the local Pastor, and the annual staff retreat. I also began to work with Elishba and Mukhtar, and my relationship with the two young women grew. Together we planned their schedule in the hospital. They also visited former patients in their homes. Once or twice a week we went out together.

Because I was older and a "memsahib," I knew that they would be inclined to defer to me in decisions rather than tell me what they really thought. I learned to present my ideas in the form of questions. We prayed together several times a week, and I usually let them decide who we might visit. We never planned these visits until just before we went out. By that time many of our friends had phones, and we had only recently gotten a phone at our home. But unlike America, where we felt we had to call before visiting, Pakistanis never expected that.

Our visits usually took place in the late morning when the women were finished with their morning chores and had not yet begun to cook dinner. This was a good time to just stop and enjoy a visit from anyone who might drop in. More formal visits took place in the late afternoon. But these casual drop-in times became very special. After entering the courtyard, we would be invited to sit on one of the *charpais*, rope strung beds, in the sun in the winter cool season, in the shade or inside the house when it was hot. Some of the women recognized us from the hospital and others were introduced. In most homes there would be one or two older women, one or more daughters-in-law, and perhaps an unmarried daughter of the family. Older children were in school but usually there were toddlers or babies.

Our conversations varied but inevitably some problem would come up. I noticed that the older women often took me aside to talk of some concern, perhaps a son's wife who was having trouble getting pregnant. The younger women tended to open up to Elishba or Mukhtar. We always prayed specifically before leaving the hospital that God would guide our conversations, so we were relaxed, leaving it to the Holy Spirit. Mukhtar had a quiet, winsome way of bringing God and His Word into the conversation. Our purpose was to plant seeds through our friendship. Often we had opportunities to talk of Jesus and our faith as they told us about their Muslim beliefs about Jesus.

One year in the fall we began to discuss what we might do to share the Christmas message of Jesus' birth with these Muslim women. At times we had organized a drama of the Christmas story. The Christians all liked this, but not many Muslims attended. Perhaps we could plan a program with scripture and song. The nurses sang well and loved to sing Christmas songs. We would use the Sindhi scriptures and songs in Urdu. We would invite them to my home and combine it with a Christmas tea party, pushing the furniture back in our huge living room and covering the tile floor with carpets so that quite a large crowd could sit on the floor. We set a date in the middle of December and began to make our plans.

As the time drew near Elishba, Mukhtar and I drew up a list and they wrote out invitations by hand. I offered Rafiq, our man of all work to deliver them, but Mukhtar shook her head.

"No," she said, "We know where all these people live. We can take them ourselves and give a personal invitation."

When the day arrived, Rafiq and Sadorah, my faithful helpers, worked alongside me to prepare the living room. I had baked Christmas cookies, Rafiq went to the sweets bazaar to get a variety of Pakistani snacks. He would go out during the program to get the *pakoras* and *samosas,* spicy, fresh and hot. Sadorah had everything ready to make a huge pot of chai. I busied myself getting the table ready, getting out what I hoped would be enough tea cups and plates.

We had set the time for four in the afternoon, realizing people would come late. I was feeling nervous. "What if no one shows up at all?"

Or perhaps worse, what if only one or two came?

Soon after four the first ladies began to arrive, followed by the nurses from the hospital carrying their hymn books and their *dholki,* the drum they used to accompany their singing. A total of 16 women came, and even more children. We had placed some Sindhi and Urdu Christmas booklets on a table near the door and told them to take whatever they would like.

Our first celebration of Christ's birth for our Muslim women friends was a huge success. We continued this the following year and it became a tradition, with women beginning to ask us as winter approached if we would be having the party again. Each year more women came, some bringing relatives or neighbors. By the third year as I mentally counted the crowd sitting on my living room floor, I realized that we had nowhere near enough tea cups for this many. I slipped out to the kitchen where Rafiq and Sadorah were arranging the food onto platters.

"Rafiq, what can we do? We only have cups for fifty and there are at least seventy here!"

"*Allah jo shukr!* Thank God!" exclaimed Sadorah, a Muslim.

Rafiq replied, "Don't worry. I'll bring some from my house and I will ask the other neighbors if that isn't enough."

I had learned in my years in Pakistan that those who worked in our home never complained over extra work because of guests. Hospitality is so highly valued in Pakistani culture that they were glad to do whatever I asked of them. It would be a shame to our name if we weren't generous in exercising hospitality, and they would share that embarrassment.

The success of our Christmas party was largely due to Elishba and Mukhtar and their care and love for these women all through the year, in the hospital and in their homes. They took on the responsibility of organizing this program each year.

In 1988 we were planning to retire from our work in Pakistan before Christmas. We had moved out of our former house so that a young family, Rod and Donna Black with their children, could move in. We moved temporarily into the home of other co-workers who were on furlough. Donna was happy for us to hold the Christmas program in her home, and I felt it was a good opportunity for these ladies to meet her. So Donna greeted each of the women as they arrived. They chatted and greeted one another as they found places to sit on the floor. We had emptied the room of the furniture so we could spread carpets and mats right to the corners, anticipating a big crowd.

When the room was full, Donna walked to the rope bed against the wall at the front. The charpai was covered with a colorful *ajrak,* a Sindhi hand blocked cotton sheet. She sat on the bed, tucked her feet under her and opened a book. As she began to chant aloud in the Sindhi language, the crowded room was completely hushed. She was reading from a Sindhi book, "The Life of Christ in Poetry" about the birth of Jesus Christ. Sindhis love poetry and the traditional way it is chanted. Donna had learned and practiced to be able to do this. When she finished, the women were silent at first and then began to respond enthusiastically, "*Wah, Wah!* Wonderful! Awesome!"

The program proceeded with singing of Christmas carols and scripture readings in Sindhi and Urdu. The tea followed, accompanied by the noisy chatter of the women. Many of the children ran outside to play in the yard.

Later as Elishba, Mukhtar and I helped Donna put her living room back to rights, we paused to thank God for what He had done in bringing so many Sindhi women and children to hear the good news of the coming of Jesus into the world.

Less than a week later Ralph and I departed from Pakistan. A number of friends accompanied us to the airport in Sukkur thirty miles away. Among them were my dear sisters, Elishba and Mukhtar. As we hugged and said our tearful farewells, I thanked the Lord for the relationship He had allowed me to have with these very special women.

I was leaving to begin life over in America. They would continue on in the work that God had called them to at Shikarpur Christian Hospital and in the city of Shikarpur. The Lord continued to shine His light through these special women for many more years until they retired to return to their home city of Lahore.

13
Sisters I Never Knew

We often traveled by train in Pakistan. For short distances we rode in third class, for longer trips, first or second. Second class train cars were divided into compartments opening onto a corridor running through on one side. With three sets of double bunks, the six passengers sat on the lowers during the day. At bedtime each person unrolled a bedroll on the reserved bunk and hoped for a bit of sleep. Children under two traveled free and those from three to twelve, paid half price. A child under two didn't get a bunk but was expected to sleep with the mother. Older children slept two, or more to a bunk.

Although third class was usually crowded with passengers sitting on wooden benches, I have pleasant memories of such trips. One car was always set aside for women, and I preferred to travel in that car even when I traveled with my husband. It was always an adventure, and I never knew what to expect. Seeing my white face the women knew I was a foreigner even though I dressed in the same style of clothing they wore. Sometimes they started talking about me in

Sindhi, thinking I wouldn't understand. While it might have been interesting to find out what they thought of me, I preferred to interrupt them by greeting them in their own language. Sitting in close quarters for a few hours, I found the women eager to chat with me and with each other. Sometimes a woman had heard of Shikarpur Christian Hospital and assumed that I must be a doctor. Out would come the medicines and a story of the illness, either hers or her child's. I heard heart-breaking stories of losing a child, or of infertility, or of a husband taking another wife. When I remember these encounters, I think of opportunities taken or missed, to speak of my relationship with God through my faith in Jesus Christ. A conversation might begin and continue for a time, only to be interrupted when the woman reached her destination. In my many travels, in those hours spent on trains, I met so many women, their names now forgotten, their faces never seen again. They are some of the sisters I never knew.

During the monsoon season in Murree, rain sometimes continues day and night, and it is quite easy to believe in Noah's flood. At other times, the rain gives way to clear sky at sunset and begins again before dawn. Occasionally showers are interspersed with breaks of sunshine barely long enough to dry clothes outside. Monsoon dampness creeps into every corner of the house. We had to regularly wipe down suitcases and shoes or green mold would ruin them.

The monsoons also brought wild berries in sunny spots deep in the forests that cover the mountains. Hill people living in those valleys know where to find these wild black raspberries,and they learned that the foreigners who come to the hills in the summer are more than happy to buy them. I was one of their customers when I was in Murree for the Murree Christian School's summer term. I made a summer home for my children in a rented cottage. Each morning they boarded a large green school bus with the name of the school emblazoned on its side, and each afternoon I welcomed them home.

On one of those damp days between showers, I heard a voice calling from outside my door, "Strawberries, Memsahib! Fresh strawberries!"

I knew they were not strawberries, but I also knew how much we enjoyed this short berry season. I picked up a bowl from the kitchen and went to the door. There I saw a woman of indeterminate age dressed in wide, full pants, a voluminous dress and a large shawl covering her head and shoulders. Her clothes were dirty – it would have been impossible to keep clean in the rainy season – and she carried a basket filled with wild black raspberries. As she squatted down to measure out the berries with my measuring cup, I noticed that she had a dirty rag tied around one foot.

After she had filled my bowl, and we had settled on a price, I pointed to her foot and asked her what had happened. I spoke in Urdu, she knew only her hill language. Somehow she explained, and I thought I understood, that she had stepped on a sharp rock in her bare feet and had cut her foot. She allowed me to take off the dirty rag, and I saw a jagged cut on the side of her foot.

I sat her in a chair and told her to wait. I explained in Urdu, hoping she would understand enough to not just run away, that I wanted to wash her foot. I brought a basin with some warm water, a cake of soap and a clean towel. I also had clean gauze bandage and antibiotic ointment.

As I knelt before her, washing this poor woman's filthy foot, I so wished I could communicate with her. I wanted to hear her story. Where did she live? Did she have children? Grandchildren? Were they in the hills all year or did they move down to warmer valleys in the winter? I chattered in Urdu as I did my work, and she occasionally answered in her language. I don't know how much she understood me; I understood little of what she said.

I dried her foot carefully, spread ointment on a square of gauze to cover the cut, then wrapped her foot in the clean bandage. I finished by putting one of my socks over the bandage. I squeezed more ointment onto a square of waxed paper and folded it up with more of the gauze, putting it all with the other sock in a small plastic bag. She might as well have both socks, one wouldn't do me much good. I told her how important it was to keep her foot clean, that I prayed that she would get good healing with the help of Allah and in the name of Isa Masih, Jesus Christ. She in turn blessed me before she slipped her sandals back on and left to sell the rest of her berries. I watched her going up the path to the road until she was out of sight. I would never see her again.

The station platform was crowded with people even at 6am. Some waited with piles of bags and boxes to board. Others, like us, had come to meet an arriving passenger. Ralph had seen an acquaintance a short distance away on the platform, and gone off to talk with him. I looked for a bench to sit on, trying to be inconspicuous. Finding no empty seats,

I stood looking around at the colorful scene. A number of village women, some enveloped in white cotton *burkas,* eye holes covered with mesh, squatted on the platform. Others, poorer perhaps, or old enough not to have to cover, dressed in a variety of styles in brilliant colors.

I approached a group of women surrounded by a mountain of bags and bedrolls and boxes and I greeted them in Sindhi. They returned my greeting, and a tiny, wrinkled, toothless Granny began to chat. She looked up at me from amidst the baggage, her eyes bright behind her steel-rimmed glasses, her skin brown and wrinkled, her gray hair colored with henna.

"We are of the Brahui people, but we live here in Shikarpur and we are going to Noshki in Baluchistan to sacrifice to a saint, our *pir,*" she told me.

"Is he alive," I asked as I squatted down beside her.

"Oh, no. He is dead" she replied, "and we are going to sacrifice at his tomb."

"But how can he help you if he is dead?" I asked.

She shrugged, and answered, "God is merciful."

As we continued our conversation, I said, "The One I follow is alive. He gave His life as a perfect sacrifice for our sins when He died on the cross. You call Him *Isa Masih* and He is not dead! God raised Him from the dead on the third day after He died. I don't have to sacrifice animals to please God and to earn my salvation. This is a gift that God gives to everyone who believes in His Son, Isa Masih."

Just then we heard the train whistle. The whole group got up to gather their belongings and get ready to board the crowded train. I looked around for Ralph and we stood, straining to see our friend Ann amidst the arriving passengers. As Ann alighted from one of the passenger cars, I watched the tiny woman climb up into a third class car, the younger women helping her. I didn't even know her name.

As we drove away from the station with Ann, I heard the mournful sound of the train whistle in the distance as it left the station heading northwest toward the cool mountains of Baluchistan. I knew I would never see this lady again. Yet our paths had crossed on a crowded railway station platform. I felt the nearly unbearable burden of the love of God for these Brahui people, on their way to sacrifice to a dead saint. How I longed for them to know God through His Son Jesus Christ!

*W*e had come to our last few months in Pakistan. After thirty-four years in Sindh, Ralph and I were retiring. Rod and Donna Black, with their young family, had moved into the house we had occupied for the past several years. We had sold, given away, or otherwise disposed of all except what we would carry to the States with us. For these last months we were living in the home of friends while they were away.

This house, like many others in Shikarpur, was large with high ceilings. A central living-dining room connected to bedrooms and a bathroom on the right, another bedroom on the left, and a door at the back led to the kitchen. Windows of the living room and the kitchen looked out on what had once been a large empty field behind the house. That area was now filled with small huts and shanties. A new slum had sprung up almost overnight as hundreds of people had moved into the space. One small family lived their daily lives just below my kitchen window. Several times a day whenever I walked into the kitchen, I found myself gazing out the window to see what was happening in the small fenced in courtyard about fifteen feet below. The man of the house left early. He was probably a day laborer and had to be in the market at dawn in hopes of getting some kind of work for the day. A young woman, dressed in the cheap cotton *shalwar* and *kameez* of a poor villager, was sweeping the hard-packed dirt floor of her tiny courtyard. A baby was tucked snugly into a hammock hanging from the side of a *charpai*. Our house offered shade during the early morning to this little home. When the woman finished her sweeping and other chores, she brought some handwork out of the house. She settled herself on the rope bed and bent over the quilt she was working on.

I saw my new neighbor follow this same routine for several days. Early one morning, after putting water on the stove to heat for tea, I stepped over to the window as I usually did. I had begun to think that I really must find my way to this house. I wanted to meet this lady, to hear the story of how she had come to this place below my kitchen window. But our house had no back door. It was a long distance from the road. I wasn't even sure which road this group of houses opened onto. If I could find my way in, how would I ever find her house through the maze of paths between the huts?

When I pulled the curtain aside that morning and looked down, the house was empty! No *charpai* with a baby hammock hanging from its side. No woman industriously sweeping her dirt floor, or sewing on her quilt. They were gone, and it was too late. I would never meet this woman who had been my neighbor. I would never sit with her and hear her story. She had been so near to me, yet so very far away. This woman seemed to symbolize the distance—cultural, linguistic, religious—that separated me from the women who had come into my life during these years. Yet in many instances God had enabled me to break down these barriers, or rather God's Spirit had broken them down.

I thank God for those women who became sisters to me. I am rich beyond measure from their friendships. Yet I often remember the others, those met on a train journey, the Brahui lady on the railway station platform, and this neighbor who was now, suddenly gone. She seemed to symbolize all the others, so many needing to know the love of God, and I can never reach them.

I take comfort in knowing that God's Word is not bound. The Church of Jesus Christ has taken root in the arid desert of southern Pakistan. A tiny number of believers live among millions of Muslim neighbors, but they are God's lights. The Word of God is there and available to readers and non-readers through smart phones. The Bible, films and Christian songs all in the Sindhi language are there. The Holy Spirit is at work and He is doing the work through God's people and through technology, continuing to grow the church of Jesus Christ until He comes again in all His glory.

Afterword

A little girl died last night.
A few weeks ago she was a bright, mischievous, dirty-faced,
little girl who never sat still. Now she is dead, and where is she?
Her mother is crying, over and over she moans,
"God didn't do anything.
He didn't do anything."
And her granny, the dear wrinkled old lady
who stayed by her granddaughter's side all
the weeks she was sick – granny quietly sobs her hopelessness.
A mother, crying for her dead child –
"She's gone, my little Princess, my Shahazadi is gone, forever."
A granny, sobbing for the little girl who was – and is no more.
A father, stoic and hardened –
He's not supposed to cry but I saw his tears.
A grandfather –
"We've gone astray, we're on the wrong road,
and God doesn't care.
You prayed, but God doesn't care
about us."
Good Shepherd of love,
I know that You care,
You died for them to bring them out of darkness,
out of their sorrow and hopelessness
into the light of life.

(From my journal, February 22, 1983)

CPSIA information can be obtained
at www.ICGtesting.com
Printed in the USA
BVHW040810170720
583967BV00009B/194